Guilt

Margaret S. Mahler Series

This series of yearly volumes began appearing in 1991 and is based upon the panel discussions presented at the prestigious Annual Margaret Mahler Symposia held in Philadelphia. Each volume consists of three papers and their discussions presented at the most recent Symposium. A thorough introduction and a comprehensive conclusion that pulls all the material together are specially written for the book. Occasionally, one or two papers that were not presented at the meeting but represent the cutting-edge thinking on the topic are also included. While this format and organization gives these books a friendly familiarity, the books' contents vary greatly and are invariably a source of excitement and clinical enthusiasm. Volumes published so far have addressed topics as diverse as hatred and cultural differences in childhood development, extramarital affairs and sibling relationship, mourning and self psychology, and resilience and boundary violations. Among the distinguished psychoanalysts whose work has appeared in this series are Salman Akhtar, Anni Bergman, Harold Blum, Ruth Fischer, Alvin Frank, Dorothy Holmes, Otto Kernberg, Selma Kramer, Peter Neubauer, Henri Parens, Fred Pine, John Munder Ross, and Ernest Wolf, to name a few. The vantage point is always broad-based and includes developmental, clinical, and cultural variables but the end point is consistently an enhancement of the technical armamentarium of the therapist.

BOOKS BASED UPON THE MARGARET S. MAHLER SYMPOSIA

- *The Trauma of Transgression* (1991)
- *When the Body Speaks* (1992)
- *Prevention in Mental Health* (1993)
- *Mahler and Kohut* (1994)
- *The Birth of Hatred* (1995)
- *The Internal Mother* (1995)
- *Intimacy and Infidelity* (1996)
- *The Seasons of Life* (1997)
- *The Colors of Childhood* (1998)
- *Thicker Than Blood* (1999)
- *Does God Help?* (2000)

- *Three Faces of Mourning* (2001)
- *Real and Imaginary Fathers* (2004)
- *The Language of Emotions* (2005)
- *Interpersonal Boundaries* (2006)
- *Listening to Others* (2007)
- *The Unbroken Soul* (2008)
- *Lying, Cheating, and Carrying On* (2009)
- *The Wound of Mortality* (2010)
- *The Electrified Mind* (2011)
- *The Mother and Her Child* (2012)
- *Guilt* (2013)

Guilt

Origins, Manifestations, and Management

Edited by Salman Akhtar

JASON ARONSON
Lanham • Boulder • New York • Toronto • Plymouth, UK

Published by Jason Aronson
A wholly owned subsidiary of The Rowman & Littlefield Publishing Group, Inc.
4501 Forbes Boulevard, Suite 200, Lanham, Maryland 20706
www.rowman.com

10 Thornbury Road, Plymouth PL6 7PP, United Kingdom

British Library Cataloguing in Publication Information Available

Library of Congress Cataloging-in-Publication Data
Guilt : origins, manifestations, and management / edited by Salman Akhtar.
pages cm. -- (Margaret Mahler series)
Includes bibliographical references and index.
ISBN 978-0-7657-0899-1 (cloth : alk. paper) -- ISBN 978-0-7657-0900-4 (electronic)
Psychotherapy. I. Akhtar, Salman, 1946 July 31- editor of compilation.
BF575.G8G84 2013
152.4'4--dc23
2012037809
ISBN 978-1-4422-4781-9 (pbk: alk. paper)

To
the memory of
MARGARET MAHLER & SELMA KRAMER
with respect and affection

Contents

Acknowledgments

The chapters in this book, with the exception of chapters 1 and 8, were originally presented as papers at the 43rd Annual Margaret S. Mahler Symposium on Child Development, held on April 28, 2012, in Philadelphia, PA. First and foremost, therefore, I wish to express gratitude to the Department of Psychiatry of Jefferson Medical College, the main sponsor of this event. I am especially indebted to Dr. Michael Vergare, Chairman of the Department of Psychiatry and Human Behavior of the Jefferson Medical College; Bernard Friedberg, President of the Psychoanalytic Foundation of the Psychoanalytic Center of Philadelphia; and William Singletary, President of the Margaret S. Mahler Foundation for their kind support. There are many others who helped in subtle and not-so-subtle ways. To them, my most sincere thanks indeed. Finally, I wish to acknowledge my deep appreciation of Ms. Jan Wright, for her superb organization of the Symposium and for her skillful preparation of this book's manuscript.

ONE

Guilt: An Introductory Overview

Salman Akhtar, M.D.

"I am sorry" is perhaps the most versatile combination of three words in the English language. Compared to its lexical rival, "I love you," the expression "I am sorry" is used far more often and in much more varied contexts. It can carry the hues of emotions that vary from flimsy courtesy through considerable remorse to soul-wrenching contrition. It can therefore be spoken with comparable ease at spilling coffee on the tablecloth, forgetting to turn the cell phone off during a play, hurting a lover's feelings, and hearing the news of someone's passing away. It can also be used by a child molester seeking a lesser punishment in a court of law, a politician caught embezzling party funds, and even a head of state expressing 'regret' for policies that led to abuses of an ethnic minority or for a weak response to a natural disaster.

All these instances involve the experience of guilt, be it real or pretended, mild or severe, fleeting or sustained. The utterance of "I am sorry" is always motivated by guilt. But what is guilt? What gives rise to it? How does it affect us? And why do some people feel so much guilt, others so little? Certainly the emotion does not result solely from committing 'bad' (i.e., hurtful) acts. If that were the case, hardened criminals and psychopaths would be enormously guilt-ridden and law-abiding citizens would be devoid of the inner naggings of conscience. Actually the opposite is true. The one who commits crimes and breaks the law is often free of remorse while the one who avoids moral and ethical transgressions frequently suffers from the pangs of guilt. The relationship between 'bad' actions and guilt therefore seems highly tenuous. It seems best, therefore, to start our investigation by defining the terms involved in it.

1

THE EXPERIENCE OF GUILT

According to the Webster's dictionary, the word 'guilt' stands for "1. The fact of having committed a breach of conduct, especially violating law and involving a penalty; 2a. The state of one who has committed an offense, especially consciously, and, 2b. Feelings of culpability, especially from imagined offenses or from a sense of inadequacy" (Mish, 1998, p. 517). The scope of this definition is broad. It includes (i) an act of breaking rules, (ii) the possibility that such act only took place in the imagination, and (iii) the emotional state of the one who has committed the transgression. Additionally, by mentioning culpability from a 'sense of inadequacy,' the dictionary definition acknowledges that acts of omission can also underlie feelings of guilt. This is pure and simple English.

That said, we turn to the five prominent psychoanalytic glossaries. Two of these (Eidelberg, 1968; Laplanche and Pontalis, 1973) do not have entries on 'guilt.' The other three do a variable job in defining guilt. Rycroft (1968) regards it to be "the emotion which follows infringement of a moral injunction" (p. 59). He adds that guilt differs from anxiety insofar as

> (a) anxiety is experienced in relation to a feared future occurrence, while guilt is experienced in relation to an act already committed, and (b) the capacity to experience guilt is contingent on the capacity to internalize objects whereas the capacity to experience anxiety is not; animals and infants may feel anxious, but only human beings with some awareness of time and of others can feel guilty. (p. 60)

Moore and Fine (1990) offer the following passage by way of defining guilt.

> Refers, like shame to a group of affects, including fear of retribution both from outside and within the self, feelings of remorse, contrition, and penitence. Its core is a form of anxiety with the underlying ideational content: "If I hurt somebody else, I shall be hurt in turn." In addition to this outer or inner retaliation for one's sexual or aggressive acts or wishes, one may hold the depressive connection that one has already hurt the other and is being punished for it; therewith goes the hope that, by atonement through mental or physical suffering, one can attain forgiveness, that is, regain love and acceptance. (p. 83)

Impressive at first glance, both of these definitions are replete with problems. Both make inadequate distinction between guilt and remorse. In addition, Rycroft leaves no space for imaginary crimes and Moore and Fine equate guilt with the fear of punishment (which is usually a consequence of guilt). The latter also do not make it explicit that the 'sexual or aggressive acts' stirring up guilt are only those prohibited by the society (and, its internal representative, the superego) and not of any and all varieties. Avoiding the excessive zeal of Moore and Fine's definition, I opted in my own *Comprehensive Dictionary of Psychoanalysis* (2009) for a more modest approach and described guilt as: "a dysphoric experience felt at breaking rules (familiar, religious, national, etc.) or even at the thought of committing such a transgression" (p. 126). By restricting the use of the word 'guilt' to the gnawing unease felt at a real or imaginary infraction, I prepared the ground for demarcating the boundaries of guilt from phenomena that are often lumped together with it.

RELATIONSHIP TO SHAME, REMORSE, AND REGRET

It is commonplace to come across discussions of guilt—psychoanalytic or otherwise—that belabor the distinctions between guilt and shame, but pay little attention to the ways in which guilt differs from remorse and regret. In the following passages, I will attempt to rectify this omission and address the overlap of guilt with all three emotions.

Guilt and Shame

The literature on the shame-guilt overlap is voluminous (e.g., Grinker, 1955; Levin, 1967; Spero, 1984; Morrison, 1989; Abrams, 1990; Wurmser, 1994; and Kilbourne, 2005) and can hardly be summarized here. The contributors have variable emphases, separate theoretical perspectives, and different descriptive nuances. However, most contributors seem to agree upon certain similarities and certain differences between the two phenomena. As far as the similarities are concerned, both affects are seen as dysphoric. Both lower self-esteem. And both work as guarantors of 'appropriate' behavior. As far as differences are concerned, the following are frequently mentioned: (i) shame is predominantly visual while guilt is predominantly auditory; (ii) the experience of shame is often accompanied by physiological markers (e.g., blushing, palpitation) while the experience of guilt is not; (iii) shame results from the rupture of self-continuity consequent upon psychomotor or social clumsiness or loss of control (e.g., belching, farting in public); guilt results from actual or imaginary breaking of societal and internalized rules (e.g., going through a red light); (iv) in structural terms, shame results from falling far behind one's wished-for self-image and one's ego ideal, while guilt results from violating the dictates of one's superego; (v) shame pushes for hiding; guilt pushes for confession; (vi) shame is developmentally earlier than guilt; the latter, in its true meaning only evolves after the post-oedipal consolidation of superego; and (vii) defenses against shame include narcissistic self-inflation, withdrawal, or turning passive into active by shaming others; defenses against guilt include blaming others, fearing external punishment, and masochistic self-laceration.

Guilt and Remorse

Guilt is a nagging unpleasant feeling of being morally questionable. It arises from harboring conscious or unconscious impulses to commit acts that are prohibited by one's religion, family traditions, local law, and, in the internalized form of all these, by the superego. In the end, guilt is about breaking rules, regardless of whether such transgressions actually take place or remain confined to the imagination. Remorse is an unpleasant and burdensome affect as well. It, too, makes one feel 'bad.' However, there are important differences between guilt and remorse. Guilt is about breaking rules and remorse about hurting others. Guilt is diminished by confession, remorse by making reparation. Guilt can be about past, present, or future; one can feel reprehensible for having broken rules, in the midst of breaking rules, and at wanting to break rules. Remorse is always about the past. It is a dysphoria that arises after one realizes (and truly acknowledges) that one has hurt someone innocent, or worse, a loved one. Guilt is the sister of anxiety, remorse a cousin of regret.

The psychoanalyst whose work is of greatest significance to the experience of remorse is Melanie Klein. While using the terms 'guilt' and 'remorse' interchangeably, Klein (1937) described the childhood origins of the latter emotion in eloquent details.

> When a baby feels frustrated at the breast, in his phantasies he attacks this breast; but if he is being gratified by the breast, he loves it and has phantasies of a pleasant kind in relation to it. In his aggressive phantasies he wishes to bite up and tear up his mother and her breasts, and to destroy her also in other ways. A most important feature of these destructive phantasies, which are tantamount to death wishes, is that the baby feels that what he desires in his phantasies has really taken place; that is to say he feels that he *has really destroyed* the object of his destructive impulses . . . in the baby's mind the conflicts between love and hate then arise, and the fears of losing the loved one become active. These feelings of guilt and distress now enter as a new element into the emotion of love. . . . Side-by-side with the destructive impulses in the unconscious both of the child and of the adult, there exists a profound urge to make sacrifices, in order to help and put right loved people who in phantasy have been harmed or destroyed. (pp. 308, 311)

As this passage demonstrates, Klein's views deftly portray the genesis of destructive impulses, fantasies of having destroyed the love object, subsequent feelings of remorse, and the impulses of reparation emanating from these.

Guilt and Regret

Guilt due to having broken rules (established by religion, law, and society) is often accompanied by wistfulness. One yearns to undo the act, desperately wishes that one had not done it. And it is at this phenomeno-logical juncture that guilt begins to have similarities with regret. Guilt about past transgressions and regret are both about events that have already taken place. Seen this way, regret is even closer to remorse since the latter is always about something in the (remote or near) past. Com-menting upon this, I have elsewhere noted (2009) that both regret and remorse

> . . . are about the past. Both are about one's own actions. Both can involve acts of commission or omission. Both lead to a wistful rumina-tion to somehow erase or undo the events of the past. Both can, there-fore, underlie the "if only . . . fantasy" (Akhtar, 1996). This fantasy assumes that, in the absence of this or that "calamity," everything would have turned out all right. Both "regret" and "remorse" can im-poverish the ego and contribute to anhedonia, depression, and suicidal tendencies. Finally, both "regret" and "remorse" can serve screen func-tions and both can be put to secondary (e.g. sadomasochistic) uses. However, there is one very important difference between the two emo-tions: "remorse" involves feelings about how one's actions have af-fected others, while "regret" involves feelings about how one's actions affected oneself. In other words, "remorse" is more object related, "re-gret" more narcissistic. (p. 244)

Two caveats must be entered to the foregoing portrayal of guilt: (i) the description focuses upon the conscious manifestations of guilt. The fact is that clinically significant guilt generally exists on an unconscious level. It is discerned through various derivative phenomena including self-deni-gration, self-destructive behavior, inhibitions of assertiveness and sexual-ity, inability to accept compliments, provocative actions to incite punish-ment, and the phenomenon of 'success neurosis' (Freud, 1914b; Holmes, 2006), and (ii) in real-life, distinctions between guilt, remorse, and regret often get blurred. This is because the three can coexist. Guilt might cause inhibitions of ego functions and the consequent failure to act appropriate-ly in a given situation might lead to shame. Breaking a rule ordinarily gives rise to guilt but if it leads to a loved one getting hurt, remorse may also follow. Remorse over hurting others might be associated with regret over one's characterological proclivities. And so on.

ORIGINS OF GUILT

The search for *font origio* of guilt leads us to two registers. One is made up of ubiquitous events and experiences of childhood. The other is consti-tuted by occurrences that might be common enough but by no means are ubiquitous. The first category leads to (i) annihilation guilt, (ii) epistemic guilt, and (iii) oedipal guilt. The second category leads to (i) separation guilt, (ii) induced guilt, (iii) deposited guilt, and (iv) survivors' guilt.

Annihilation Guilt

During childhood, our desires are simple, direct, and intolerant of delay in their gratification. We want what we want; we despise realities and people who come in the way of the fulfillment of our wishes. We wish such 'enemies' gone, vanished, even dead. We wish to annihilate them. Given the limited circumference of our childhood interpersonal world, it is our parents and siblings who usually constitute such 'enemies.'[1] They are the ones who seem to come in the way of the immediate gratification of our wishes. No wonder we hate them from time to time and, in the typical childhood more of absolutism, wish them dead. And it is the persistence of these death wishes toward others that becomes the bedrock of the human experience of guilt. Unlike 'annihilation anxiety' (for a formidable survey of literature on this topic, see Hurvich, 2003), which is the distress felt due to the anticipated disintegration of the self, 'annihilation guilt' is the distress felt at the self-caused destruction of one's love objects.

Epistemic Guilt

An additional source of guilt is formed by our childhood curiosities and their uninhibited expression. As children, we ask questions that seem natural to us (e.g., "why does grandpa smell of pee all the time?" "wouldn't Aunt Jenny die if she smokes?") but make adults around us uncomfortable. At other times, even mundane questions of ours (e.g., "Dad, what time are we going out?") are responded to by our parents (especially if they are tired, hungover, sick, worried, etc.) with annoyance and disapproval. In either case, we are silenced. But the questions—and the wish to ask them aloud—remain alive within us. And since we have internalized the adult injunctions, it makes us feel bad. This is 'epistemic guilt.'[2]

One special form of it pertains to our sexual curiosities and all sorts of 'naughty' prying into our parents' privacy caused by them. Remember how, as children, we fearfully but fervently tried to figure out the mysteries of sexuality? How do babies come into a mother's 'tummy'? What are the penis and vagina actually meant to do? What is this thing called 'sex'? Is it pleasurable or painful? Do our parents really 'do it'? Such questions and the accompanying sense—caused by the parental reaction of disapproval—that there is something wrong about entertaining them preoccupied us. This, too, forms an important layer to the bedrock of guilt in all of us.

Oedipal Guilt

When the 'annihilation guilt' and 'epistemic guilt' occur in the context of early triadic relations within the family, the resulting phenomenon is called 'oedipal guilt.' Here, the importance of Freud's (1913, 1914, 1916, 1917, 1924a) observations is paramount. He emphasized that "parricide and incest with the mother are the two great human crimes" (1916, p. 333) and that the sense of guilt derived from the Oedipus complex was a reaction to "the criminal intentions of killing the father and having sexual relations with the mother" (1916, p. 333). The gender-bias implicit in these pronouncements (i.e., matricide and incest with the father being overlooked) was more or less corrected in some of his other writings (see especially 1917, p. 333-334). Freud's main point, however, remained that the erotically driven wishes to woo the opposite-sex parent and eliminate the same-sex parent form the essence of Oedipus complex, and the persistence of such wishes in the unconscious (despite their overt renunciation due to parental disapproval and, later, superego threat) forms a source of lifelong vulnerability to guilt. The greater the strength of such unconscious wishes, the greater the amount of guilt. Success in life's pursuits then gets equated with oedipal victory and mobilizes guilt. Indeed, some individuals are "wrecked by success" (1916, p. 316) and a few others become "criminal from a sense of guilt" (1916, p. 332), that is, arrange to get punished by conscious misdeeds as an expiation for transgressive impulses in the unconscious. Freud's earlier (1913b) proposal of an actual, even if 'pre-historic,' murder of the primal father having saddled man with ancestral 'badness' had a similar oedipal ring to it.

Separation Guilt

The feelings of 'wrongdoing' that narcissistic and needy parents inculcate in their children when the latter begin to take steps toward psychic autonomy and independence can be meaningfully termed 'separation guilt.' Here the child's ego advances are age-specific and maturationally appropriate but are rendered doubt-ridden and 'bad' by the parental response to them. Following Pine's (1997) useful distinction between 'separation anxiety' and 'separateness anxiety,'[3] perhaps it is better to call the feeling under question 'separateness guilt.' Regardless of which label one uses, this sort of guilt is seen more often in children raised by self-centered, sickly, lonely, and otherwise needy parents. Children of immigrant parents often find themselves in the role of their parents' teachers and therefore feel guilty in developing their own identities and independent lives (Akhtar and Choi, 2004).

Induced Guilt

A related phenomenon is 'induced guilt.' This refers to the feeling of 'badness' that arises in a child when the parents vociferously announce the suffering they have undergone in raising him. For instance, mothers who repeatedly tell their child about the difficulties in her pregnancy and labor ("you know, when you were born, I bled so much that I nearly died") end up burdening him with profound guilt (Asch, 1976). Similarly, immigrant parents who parade their culturally dislocated lives as a sacrifice for their offspring ("we are not of this country and we do not really fit here but we live here so that you can have a better life") cause the latter to suffer enormous amounts of guilt.

Deposited Guilt

This type of guilt results from the child's succumbing to the 'projective identification' (Klein, 1935; Kernberg, 1975) of their parents' guilt. In other words, parents feel guilty about something and cannot bear it. They split their guilt-ridden self-representations off and deposit them in their child. Then they subtly manipulate him to live these attributes out. An illustration is formed by a father who feels guilty about being more affluent than his own father; he can ward off this intrapsychic burden by constantly criticizing his son for every little transgression of family rules. Repeated over a long period of time, especially during the formative years of childhood, such 'depositing' (Volkan, 1987) results in a son who is chronically guilt-ridden due to no fault of his own.

Survivors' Guilt

This type of guilt was originally described in the context of Holocaust survivors who suffer from lifelong anguish over their escaping the fatal blow that fell upon their friends and family members (Niederland, 1968). It is also seen in those who have outlived comrades killed in combat and loved ones in accidents. Individuals whose parents died during their childhood and individuals raised with a grossly impaired sibling are vulnerable to 'survivors' guilt' as well. The death of a child almost invariably leaves a residue of such guilt in his or her parents. One variable that might determine the intensity of guilt in such situations is whether the avoidance of ill fortune is the result of an active decision made by the survivor or due to mere happenstance (Mark Moore, personal communication, 3 April 2008).

Extending Niederland's ideas further, Modell (1965) proposed that a sense of guilt can be precipitated by "the awareness that one has something more than someone else. This sense of guilt is invariable accompanied by a thought, which may remain unconscious, that what one has obtained is at the expense of taking something away from somebody else" (p. 328). This sort of guilt might get condensed with other sources of pre-oedipal or oedipal guilt but remains a dynamic entity unto itself.

Having elucidated the various origins of guilt, we can move on to the consequences of guilt. The question, 'what causes guilt?' has a counterpoint, i.e., 'what does guilt cause?'

CONSEQUENCES OF GUILT

Feelings of guilt—and remorse—can exert considerable influence upon the course of an individual's life. The impact is greater if the guilt is excessive, the ego is weak, and access to receiving forgiveness (for guilt) and making reparation (for remorse) is blocked. Moreover, bearable amounts of guilt and remorse, especially when existing on a conscious level, are more amenable to productive outcomes. Unconscious guilt, in contrast, is vulnerable to defensive distortions that, in turn, lead to maladaptive behavior patterns. In clinical practice such outcomes appear to result from (i) projection of blame, (ii) externalization of the punishing agency, and (iii) libidinization of suffering, leading to masochism and self-punishment. A fourth and far more fortunate outcome is seeking forgiveness and offering reparation.

Projection of Blame

Guilt is often warded off by attributing blame to others. By irritable nit-picking, the guilty individual shifts the burden of contrition to someone else. Finding faults in others relieves him of self-criticism. Paranoia thus becomes a useful defense against depressive anxieties. In his elucidation of the relationship between guilt and hate, Jones (1929) made the following astute observation.

> Hatred for someone implies that the other person, through his cruelty or unkindness, is the cause of one's sufferings, that the latter are not self-imposed or in any way one's own fault. All the responsibility for the misery produced by unconscious guilt is thus displaced on to the other, supposedly cruel person, who is therefore heartily hated. The mechanism is, of course, very familiar in the transference situation. We know that behind it there always lies guilt, but further analysis still shows, in my opinion always, that the guilt itself is dependent on a still deeper and quite unconscious layer of hate, one that differs strikingly from the top layer in not being ego-syntonic. (p. 384)

Clinically, this is evident in patients who chronically complain about others' behavior while overlooking their own role in provoking such mistreatment. Societally, this mechanism is responsible for political leaders blaming 'outsiders' for problems of their people while ignoring the ways in which they themselves have contributed to these problems. The Osama bin Laden—George Bush diatribe is a case in point. Osama bin Laden held Western, particularly North American, cultural imperialism and political hegemony responsible for the turmoil in the Islamic world, taking little notice of how the corrupt and autocratic leaders of Muslim nations were equally, if not more, responsible for the crises there. George Bush, a pro at externalization himself, put the blame of America's problems on Muslims 'out there' who simply did not like 'our way of life' and were out to destroy it; he closed his eyes to how the policies of the U.S. government themselves were corroding the fabric of education, health care, and employment opportunities in the nation. Bin Laden blamed the West; Bush blamed the East. Neither were willing (or able) to look at their own dismal records.

Externalization of the Punishing Agency

Another pathological consequence of unconscious guilt is that it undergoes externalization and gives rise to undue fears of adverse occurrences (Jones, 1929). The dread might remain diffuse and create all sorts of doom and gloom scenarios in the mind. Or it might be focused upon authority figures. Employers, policemen, and individuals in positions of power then begin to appear too intimidating. One lives a life of fear and avoidance, though unconscious hostility toward authority figures (the original cause of guilt) often breaks through and serves as an agent provocateur of punishment. Locating this dynamic within the oedipal context, Jones (1929) observed that:

> If the self-punishing tendencies are at all highly developed, we may expect to find that the patient will provoke the outer world, i.e. father-substitutes, to inflict punishments on him, and it is easy to see that this is done in order to diminish the sense of guilt; by provoking external punishment the patient saves himself from some of the severity of internal (self-) punishment. We get three layers very alike to the other sets of three mentioned above: first dread of external punishment (e.g. by the father); then guilt and self-punishment to protect the personality from the outer one, the method of religious penance; and finally, the evoking of external punishment, a disguised form of the original one, so as to protect the personality from the severity of the self-punishing tendencies. (p. 386)

Libidinization of Suffering

This is perhaps the most common manifestation of guilt in clinical practice. Guilt gives rise to a need for punishment and to masochism which satisfies this need. Since this is a realm of great clinical importance, it might not be bad to look into the 'need for punishment' and 'masochism' concepts a bit more carefully.

Sigmund Freud's ideas about what he called the 'need for punishment' evolved in four steps: (i) in 1909, he noted that the self-reproaches of the obsessional neurotic were forms of self-punishment; (ii) in 1916, he described a character type called 'criminal from a sense of guilt'; this constellation involved committing outrageous and socially unacceptable, even criminal, acts in order to elicit punishment and relieve unconscious guilt; (iii) in 1923, he described the phenomenon of 'negative therapeutic reaction' whereby the analysand responds adversely to a correct interpretation, thus betraying his difficulty with improvement; this, too, is an evidence of unconscious guilt; and (iv) in 1924(a), he talked about how the 'need for punishment' can become sexualized. What was an attempt to seek superego retribution now turns into an instinctual gratification itself.

Such gratification is subsumed under the concept of 'masochism.' A term coined by von Krafft-Ebing (1892) as a generalization for the erotic role of pain and humiliation in the novels of Von SacherMasoch, 'masochism' consists of being dominated, controlled, hurt, and humiliated by a person of the opposite sex for the purpose of erotic gratification. This narrow definition led to Freud's (1905, 1915, 1919, 1920, 1924b) wide-ranging ideas about masochism. The trajectory of these speculations dovetails the evolution of his instinct theory in general and the oedipal situation in particular. To begin with, Freud (1905) regarded sadism and masochism as component instincts of sexuality and declared that they invariably coexisted; it was thus heuristically better to speak of sadomasochism than of sadism and masochism alone. In his first dual instinct theory, Freud (1905, 1915) regarded sadism—a pleasurable infliction of pain upon others—as primary and masochism as secondary (being a deflection of sadism upon the self). In his second dual instinct theory, Freud (1920) proposed that masochism was a manifestation of death instinct; it was primary, and sadism, its outward deflection, was secondary. In these and other papers (e.g., 1919, 1924b), Freud related masochism to the fantasy of being beaten by the father and saw it as providing both sexual satisfaction and punishment for one's forbidden wishes. He thus introduced the intricate relationship masochism has with guilt and divided masochism into three types: (i) *primary*, which was the somatic substrate of death instinct bound with the libido of life instinct; the pleasure in pain came from the latter source; (ii) *erotic* or *feminine*, which was the attitude underlying sexually exciting fantasies in men of being bound, beaten, and humiliated,[4] and (iii) *moral*, which emanated from an unconscious sense of guilt and led to chronic self-depreciation and self punishment. Analytic investigators following Freud (e.g., Berliner, 1958; Brenner, 1959; Bergler, 1961) elaborated, elucidated, and expanded the meanings of the term 'masochism.' This led, on the one hand, to increasing sophistication of understanding, and, on the other hand, to the term 'masochism' acquiring "a confusing array of meanings and connotations drawn from varied levels of abstraction . . . [which] may falsely suggest underlying similarity between fundamentally different phenomena" (Maleson, 1984, p. 325).

A natural corollary of the evolving psychoanalytic ideas on masochism was the concept of 'masochistic character.' While a large number of analysts have contributed to its understanding, the views of the following seem most prominent: Reich (1933) proposed that 'masochistic character' arose out of severe childhood frustrations; much aggression was mobilized, but, instead of being discharged on frustrating others, was defensively directed at oneself; individuals with a 'masochistic character' were passive-aggressive, guilt-inducing, and coercive in their demand for love. Berliner (1958) sidelined the instinctual basis of masochism and emphasized its object-relational value. Masochism, for him, was a child's way to cope with his sadistic parents. The masochist mistreated himself and sought mistreatment by others because his superego was patterned after his cruel parents; love of suffering was an adaptive response to an abnormal childhood environment. Brenner (1959), in contrast, declared that masochism represented the acceptance of a painful penalty for forbidden sexual pleasures associated with oedipal fantasies. Bergler (1961) saw masochism as "a desperate attempt to maintain infantile megalomania" (p. 18). The masochist unconsciously provokes and enjoys rejection but consciously reacts with righteous indignation. This helps him deny his responsibility in the rejection and his unconscious pleasure in it. After the outburst of pseudo-aggression, he indulges in self-pity and unconsciously enjoys the wound-licking. And Cooper (1988), who highlighted the coexistence of narcissism and masochism, proposed the concept of 'narcissistic-masochistic character.' Individuals with such psychopathology seek suffering for their instinctual excesses and find justification for these excesses in their suffering.

Seeking Forgiveness and Offering Reparation

An outcome of guilt healthier than those described above (projection, externalization, and libidinization) consists of seeking forgiveness and offering reparation. Acknowledging one's misdeeds and apologizing for them improves reality testing, diminishes the need for projection and externalization, and enhances the possibility of being forgiven (Akhtar, 2002).[5] It also raises the self-esteem of the victim and goes a long way in repairing the damage to the relationship. Offering reparation diminishes remorse especially if it is preceded by a genuine apology. Reparation in the absence of apology belies 'manic defense' (Klein, 1935) and can deepen the psychic wound of the victim.

The principle of 'doing good' to undo the 'bad' also undergirds the rehabilitative dimension of the justice system. Guilt and remorse are washed away by years of good conduct (even if it is done behind bars) and the damaged internal objects can be more or less restored by acknowledgment of wrongdoing, apology, reparation, and reformed behavior. Often matters do not need to go this far and a guilty individual is able to 'balance' his inner sense of unworthiness by devotion to civic service and philanthropy.

CONCLUDING REMARKS

In this introductory overview, I have described the subjective experience of guilt and distinguished it from the related phenomena of shame, remorse, and regret. I have traced the origins of guilt to infantile and childhood aggressive and hostile impulses, both outside of and within the oedipal context. I have tried to show that Klein's work is more pertinent to pre-oedipal remorse and the consequent drive of reparation while Freud's work is more pertinent to oedipal guilt and the consequent need for punishment. In addition, I have noted that seeds of lifelong guilt can be sown by parental proclamations of suffering and sacrifice on behalf of their children, by parental depositing of their own unresolved guilt into the children's psyche, by parental intolerance of their children's developmentally appropriate strivings for autonomy, and by accidents of nature and random occurrences that leave the individual in a more fortunate position than his loved ones. Finally, I have delineated three pathological outcomes (projection, externalization, and libidinization) and one healthy (apology and reparation) outcome of guilt.

Despite casting a wide net, I have not been able to address two important issues, namely, the impact of gender and of culture upon the experience of guilt. Both variables demand attention but the burgeoning literature on these topics defies a quick summarization here. Suffice it to say that (i) it is conceivable that some cultures (e.g., Japan) are more driven by shame (Kitayama, 1997) and others by guilt, (ii) the high rate of suicide in Germany, Austria, Japan, and Switzerland and the low rate of suicide in Holland, Italy, Brazil, and Spain (Weiss, 1974) make one wonder about the culturally determined vulnerability to guilt and self-punishment, and (iii) in a sharp rebuttal to Freud's (1923, 1925) denigration of women's morality, recent studies (Gilligan, 1982; Bernstein, 1983) have found differences in the nature, not in the strength, of the female superego when compared to its male counterpart. The relevance of such culture-based and gender-specific insights to the understanding of guilt in its clinical and non-clinical dimensions is indeed great and needs to be pursued further.

Attention also needs to be paid to the technical handling of guilt as it emerges during clinical sessions. Generally speaking, one encounters the derivative forms of guilt (e.g., blaming others, negative therapeutic reaction) more often than explicit self-accusation. The latter, in fact, are more reflective of non-guilt-based self-hatred and sadomasochism than of guilt *per se*. Technical approaches to such problems—and other clinical vicissitudes of guilt—vary in accordance to the analyst's theory, the stage of treatment, and the particular relational and communicative idiosyncrasies of the specific dyad. In general, a multi-pronged strategy seems best, especially if it takes the following six factors into account: (i) interpretation of the defenses against the awareness of guilt, (ii) interpretation of the defenses against the awareness of the masochistic pleasure drawn from guilt, (iii) interpretation of the unconscious sadistic aspects of chronic self-blaming, especially in the context of transference, (iv) reconstruction of the sources of guilt, (v) interpretation of defensive functions of guilt (e.g., against lack of omnipotence in those who have lost parents as children), and (vi) help with bearing some guilt and finding productive ways of dealing with it.

NOTES

1. Freud (1917) notes that while murderous impulses are a regular component of the childhood oedipal experience, such wishes are even more strongly felt and verbalized in the context of the sibling relationship.

2. The biblical tale of Adam and Eve is an illustration *par excellence* of such 'epistemic guilt.'

3. Pine emphasizes that all anxiety at separation is not 'separation anxiety.' For instance, a patient who feels anxious upon learning of his analyst's vacation may be responding to a drive upsurge consequent upon the removal of an externalized superego. Or he may be responding to an anticipated disorganization of the self. The former anxiety, while precipitated by separation, is not true 'separation anxiety,' since the separation in question is from a well-differentiated object. True 'separation anxiety' involves a relationship with an undifferentiated other and is therefore an "anxiety over the sense of separateness" (1997, p. 230). This is better termed 'separateness anxiety.'

4. The fact that all the cases from which Freud drew the idea of 'feminine' masochism were males betrays a certain rigid preconception of theorizing.

5. This is distinct from the syndrome of 'relentless forgiveness seeking' (Akhtar, 2002). Individuals with such a malady are relentlessly apologetic about ordinary errors of daily life. They betray a heavy burden of unconscious guilt. Apologizing for their actions does not relieve them of the prohibited and morally repugnant hostile and sexual intentions that lurk in their unconscious. However, the act of repeatedly seeking pardon itself can come to have hostile aims and a hidden sexual discharge value.

TWO

Pinocchio's Journey to a 'Good Heart': Guilt, Reparation, and Transformation

William Singletary, M.D.

Written by Carlo Collodi in 1883, the story of Pinocchio's transformation from a wooden puppet to a flesh-and-blood boy can be understood as a rich metaphor for a basic developmental process. As such, *Pinocchio* can contribute to psychoanalysis in a number of ways. Pinocchio's rite of passage elucidates a crucial growth-promoting process which helps guide progressive, adaptive development over the life span, as well as charting the therapeutic process of change. Moreover, the story can inform our understanding of therapeutic goals, as well as help us reconsider our technique. In addition, when used as a tool in therapy with patients, *Pinocchio* can provide both a moving illustration of common emotional conflicts and a guide to the process of treatment. To see some of their most well-hidden and disturbing conflicts enacted in such a popular fairy tale can help patients realize that all of us share such troubles. Finally, the story of Pinocchio demonstrates that true change is possible through the hard work of therapy. While I employ psychoanalytic concepts, this is not primarily a psychoanalytic interpretation of Pinocchio. Rather, the basic concept of a journey from emotional imprisonment to reparation and transformation is at the heart of Dante's *Divine Comedy*, definitely an influence upon Collodi (Perella, 1986).

PINOCCHIO'S JOURNEY

Pinocchio's journey to a good heart begins with efforts to develop what I refer to in treatment as a 'good' conscience and 'good' guilt, because they

15

lead to successful adaptation. This is similar to Disney's (1940, 1986) description of one of Pinocchio's tasks, "learn to choose between right and wrong" (p. 14); of Jiminy Cricket's role as Pinocchio's conscience, that is, to be his guide; and of the definition of conscience as "a still, small voice" that people should listen to (p. 16). This resembles what Roy Schafer (1960) referred to as the 'loving and beloved' superego. This 'good' conscience helps us to know the difference between right and wrong and to make growth-promoting choices, serving as a useful guide in life. We must learn to listen to this 'still, small voice,' which is not too harsh and helps us recognize our destructiveness, and feel a sad guilt.

However, like many of us, Pinocchio begins with a 'bad' conscience or hostile superego (Schafer, 1960) and its manifestation, 'bad' guilt. These promote pathological development and obstruct helpful change in therapy. This concept of the 'upside down' or bad conscience, which can seem so paradoxical at first glance, is one of Collodi's most helpful metaphors. He makes a clear distinction between inner figures like the Cricket and the Blue Fairy, who are beneficial guides, and others who, through blatant distortions, make what is bad appear good and good appear bad, tempting Pinocchio down the wrong path toward hurtful consequences (Perella, 1986). This duality has been captured in the familiar cartoon image of a person with an angel on one shoulder and a devil on the other. Children often name this part of themselves, for example, the 'Mean Queen' or the 'King of Evil,' or talk about having an evil twin (Singletary, 2000). In the story, Lampwick, the delinquent boy whom Pinocchio follows to Funland, is only one among several characters who represent a bad conscience (Perella, 1986). Lampwick seduces Pinocchio to want what is harmful and steers him toward a magical world of omnipotent control and narcissistic self-centeredness that effectively insulates him from ordinary human vulnerability. The concomitant 'bad guilt' is exaggerated and cruel, provoking fear and subsequent attacks and punishment of others as well as ourselves (Safán-Gerard, 1998; Grinberg, 1964; Grinberg, 1978). 'Good' guilt, by contrast, leads to reparation (Klein, 1940; Segal, 1974; Safán-Gerard, 1998; Grinberg, 1964; Grinberg, 1978). Pinocchio's misadventures cause his father to become seriously ill. This is an apt image of a loved and loving figure whom we have harmed, either externally through hostile verbal or physical attacks, or internally by harboring destructive distortions of their images or representations (Klein, 1957; Segal, 1974). One example of the latter is the child who turns a loving, helpful mother into a mean, spiteful mother in his mind because of her setting relatively minor limits or because of everyday disappointments. In the story, Pinocchio is guilty of hurting his father both ways— not only through his spiteful behavior but also through his misinterpretation of loving parental concern as authoritarian oppression. A concerned recognition of his destructiveness eventually leads Pinocchio to repair the damage he has done. He works hard doing farm labor to earn money for the milk his father needs to recover. His self-sacrifice triggers Pinocchio's passage from a callous puppet into a caring boy, achieved through his back-breaking, repetitive work on behalf of his father (Wurmser, 2007). His capacity to love and care—a manifestation of his newly emerging 'good' heart—wins out over his hostile self-centeredness (Guroian, 1998). Similarly, the task of therapy is to repeatedly spotlight the patient's hostile attacks on loved ones in order to foster the experience of a sad, loving guilt which opens the door to restorative reparation and emotional transformation (Safán-Gerard, 1998).

Like mythology (Armstrong, 2005), fairy tales and children's stories can be considered a form of psychology, designed to help us manage the universal challenges presented throughout the life cycle. These stories help us cope with internal crises and navigate a productive path in the face of powerful feelings, especially love, vulnerability, loss, death, and human destructiveness—the basic issues which permeate the story of Pinocchio. How do we deal with these pains of life? The story clearly juxtaposes contrasting models of helpful and unhelpful modes of emotional self-regulation. One way leads to a closed, hard-hearted, imprisoned self, and the other to an open, loving life of freedom. If we become imprisoned, how do we then become free? This is the pivotal challenge that Pinocchio faces.

PSYCHOANALYTIC GOALS AND TREATMENT

Pinocchio's quest to attain a 'good heart' is a beautiful symbol for a primary goal of psychoanalysis. In the words of Leonard Shengold: "Psychoanalysts 'cure'. . . by love—that is, by means of a healing power that depends on the patient being able to acquire or regain (and also to tolerate) a kind of love—the non-sexual empathic caring about self and other . . . (called) *caritas*" (2004, p. 29). For Shengold, love is a curative force, central to the analytic process, as well as an analytic goal, to optimize the patient's capacity to love and be loved. For example, six-year-old Bobby had experienced early deprivation that impeded his ability to tolerate deep emotional bonds. After several years in analysis he announced that I should refer to myself as a 'love doctor' because "our work is about how loving feelings get changed into hating feelings and how hating feelings get changed back to loving feelings." When a patient enters treatment, the normal developmental process which revolves around giving and receiving love has often become derailed. 'Hating feelings'—to borrow Bobby's phrase—and internal conflicts have blocked this fundamental human process. After he kicked his mother immediately following a wonderful time with her, I said to Bobby, "I think that whenever you're mean to people, it's because you're feeling more loving and caring toward them" (Hughes, 1997). Bobby smiled and replied, "I'll pay you a quarter for that." Like Pinocchio, Bobby was conflicted about giving and receiving love and needed to develop inner structures for growth-promoting emotional self-regulation.

As Settlage (1992) has proposed, psychoanalytic treatment—with adults as well as children—entails both therapeutic and developmental processes which are separate but complementary. The therapeutic process emphasizes the interpretation of conflicts and opens the patient to giving and receiving love which leads to new developmental experiences. New development leads to structural change which increases the ability to face unconscious conflicts in therapy (Settlage, 1992). The patient's hostile attacks on the therapist in response to feeling more loved and loving become a central therapeutic focus (Singletary, 2001). Fortunately, this process can be quite obvious in children, which can alert us to the adult's much more subtle attacks. For example, a five-year-old boy impulsively jumped from the top stair in my toy closet. I caught him, preventing his injury, and his response was to spit in my face! Such therapeutic work concentrates upon interpreting defenses against affect within the transference (Hoffman, 2007), especially, omnipotence and hostility as defenses against sadness and need (Bornstein, 1949). This interpretation of hatred as a reaction to feeling more love rather than as a justified reaction to hurt is a vital aspect of how "hating feelings get changed back into loving feelings." This is indispensable to the formation of 'good' guilt, whereby remorse leads to a longing for reparation.

The story of *Pinocchio* highlights aspects of the developmental process which I feel have been too often neglected in psychoanalysis—namely the therapeutic importance of courage, choice, effort, and hard work—and has critical implications for the supportive aspects of psychoanalytic technique. Courage is required to confront our fears and risk loving and being loved, a choice that ultimately promotes the development of ego strengths and the capacity for self-regulation. Consistent effort and hard work build reflective function or what I refer to in therapy as 'feelings muscles'—the ability to 'lift' or flexibly manage intense painful affects. Kerry and Jack Novick (Novick and Novick, 2012) refer to building 'emotional muscle' and have pointed out that the patient's reality-based hard work and constructive choices need to be supported by the therapist (Novick and Novick, 2003). In addition, these vital capacities represent crucial goals of analytic work. The Novicks (Novick and Novick, 2001) consider the capacity to choose to be the ultimate goal of psychoanalysis and emphasize Freud's statement that the aim of analysis is "to give the patient's ego freedom to decide one way or the other" (Freud, 1923, p. 50, cited in Novick and Novick, 2001). In addition, object constancy, a primary developmental goal as well as a major objective of treatment, seems quite similar to Pinocchio's ambition to acquire a 'good heart' (Guroian, 1998; Gaylin, 1990), to be able to experience the vulnerability and sadness associated with loving. Mahler, stating agreement with Hoffer (1955), considered object constancy to be present when "the object is still longed for, and not rejected (hated) as unsatisfactory simply because it is absent" (Mahler, Pine, and Bergman, 1975, p. 110). This process implies choice—opting to feel sad rather than resorting to defensive hatred. In addition, Blum (1996) considers object constancy to be closely associated with the benevolent superego and self-regulation, much like Pinocchio's notion of a 'good heart.'

TWO OPERATING SYSTEMS IN THE PROCESS OF DEVELOPMENT

Before examining *Pinocchio* further, I would like to return to the first part of what Bobby said to me: "Our work is about how loving feelings get changed into hating feelings," which defines the therapeutic task of understanding how experience has led to the development of excessive hostility. Of course we're all familiar with Henri Parens's (1979) important contributions concerning the development of hostility in early childhood. In addition, Selma Fraiberg (1982) considered 'fighting' to be a pathological defense developed in infancy. The analogy which I have found helpful is that of computer operating systems. Just as we can install both an Apple operating system and a Windows operating system on a Mac computer, humans are born with two operating systems for self-regulation. The first system, which the Novicks (2001, 2012) refer to as the 'open system' and which I have referred to as 'loving object constancy' (Singletary, 2000, 2005, 2007), is based on reality, competence, acceptance of loss, a helpful conscience, choice, responsibility, and effort. When the infant's early experience is dominated by safety and loving connections, the 'open system' develops and becomes the default operating system, corresponding to Pinocchio's goal of having a 'good heart' that facilitates attachment and emotional freedom. The other operating system—the 'closed system' (Novick and Novick, 2001, 2012) or 'hostile object constancy' (Singletary, 2000, 2005, 2007)—is based on magic, omnipotence, power and control in relationships, denial of need and sadness, and a destructive conscience which can be either overly punitive or lenient. When excessive danger, threat, helplessness, and aloneness dominate early experience, the 'closed system' becomes the default mechanism (Novick and Novick, 2001, 2012; Singletary, 2000, 2005, 2007), comparable to the image of imprisonment in *Pinocchio*. Just like on a computer, in life we can choose to switch back and forth between operating systems at any point, but we can run only one operating system at a time. The more we choose to use one system of self-regulation, the more that pathway becomes the default mode both psychologically and neurobiologically.

In reference to the latter, a recent development in neurobiology has been the dramatic rise in our understanding of neuroplasticity or the brain's capacity to change. According to Hebb's Law (Hebb, 1949), "neurons that fire together wire together" (cited in Doidge, 2007, p. 223). As the brain develops, connections between neurons change and stabilize based on neuronal activity. Building on this insight, Lewis (2005) describes the mechanism of 'cascading constraints,' such that early developmental structures limit the characteristics of structures that will develop later. Thus, alongside the potential for progressive, optimal development of the brain, there exists the possibility for maladaptive plasticity or pathological brain organization (Helt et al., 2008). Either the growth-promoting, open, loving system of self-regulation or the pathological closed, hating system of self-regulation comes to be the default operating system. Excessive reliance on the closed system which is opposed to adaptive development and change leads to psychological imprisonment. This is where the story of *Pinocchio* begins.

BACK TO PINOCCHIO

In the very first pages of *Pinocchio*, we encounter the theme of imprisonment, a fitting image of the closed system. When Master Cherry gives Geppetto the piece of wood destined to become the puppet, he asks, "Could someone be hidden inside it?" (Collodi, 1883, p. 87). The idea that a real person may be hidden or trapped inside a block of wood recalls Michelangelo's unfinished sculptures called 'prisoners' or 'slaves' and Dante's spiral down through *The Inferno* to the lower rungs of hell where people are frozen in ice and unable to move. Pinocchio's material captivity concretizes his emotional imprisonment; a sense of entrapment that is experienced by many patients. In *The Imprisoned Analysand*, Roy Schafer (1983) notes that imprisonment is a frequent theme in analysis. According to British analyst Herbert Rosenfeld, "it is essential to help the patient find and rescue the dependent sane part of the self from its trapped position inside the psychotic narcissistic structure" (1971, p. 175). Surprisingly, in his book, *Prisoners of Hate*, Aaron Beck (1999) addresses this same clinical problem from the perspective of cognitive therapy and considers ways this method can help free patients from their self-imposed prisons. In the initial stages of therapy, I often hear the theme of a loving self, imprisoned by defensive hatred. My approach with patients is similar to Michelangelo's thoughts about sculpture, namely that it is the work of the artist to release the statue from the block of marble that imprisons it (Blunt, 1962). Pinocchio's journey from a narcissistic puppet, trapped by his own rage (Guroian, 1998; Kohut, 1972) to a real boy with a 'good heart' maps an analogous transformation.

Collodi doesn't tell us directly how Pinocchio became trapped inside this log, but in applying a developmental perspective, Pinocchio's experience appears dominated by traumatic loss, threat, and deprivation. While watching a children's stage production of *Pinocchio,* a 2-1/2-year-old boy raised a key question, "Where's Pinocchio's mommy?" The theme of parent loss is woven throughout the story, along with ongoing threats of mutilation, starvation, poverty, and death that lurk around every corner. Pinocchio's vulnerability is highlighted in contemporary artist Jim Dine's print, *Walking With Me* (1997), which depicts Pinocchio being carried on Death's shoulders (Davis, 2007), an insightful illustration of the fear of annihilation that can lead to a closed system and emotional imprisonment.

Pinocchio begins as a hyperactive, impulsive, out-of-control child who acts without thinking. He attacks loving figures, even killing the Cricket to silence his admonitions regarding the importance of obedience and hard work. Fearing starvation without his father, he begs on the street for food, arrives home soaking wet, and burns off his feet while trying to warm them by the fire. Despite a stint in the poorhouse due to Pinocchio's antics, his forgiving father repairs the puppet and, disregarding the freezing weather, sells his only overcoat to give his recalcitrant son a schoolbook. How does Pinocchio demonstrate his gratitude? He sells the book to attend a puppet show. Rather than follow his father and, later, the Blue Fairy, Pinocchio chooses to follow the Fox and the Cat—along with other personifications of his 'bad' conscience, a self-punitive and self-destructive force that repeatedly leads him astray. Consequently, he has numerous run-ins with the law, undergoes punishment after punishment, barely escapes death, serves time in jail, and is even forced to work as a watchdog. Rather than accept responsibility for his misfortunes, Pinocchio blames others, further impeding progressive growth and development.

The process of change does not begin until after his release from jail; finally Pinocchio shows some insight. "How many bad things have happened to me! . . . But I deserve them, because I'm a stubborn and willful puppet. . . . I always want things my own way without listening to those who love me and have 1000 times more sense than I have. . . . Can there be a more ungrateful and heartless boy than I am?" (Collodi, p. 233). Pinocchio then finds what seems to be the Fairy's tombstone. Overcome by excessive remorse, a sign of incipient 'good' guilt, Pinocchio begins to deal with loss, death, and sadness as well as to recognize his own destructiveness.

After Pinocchio learns that the Fairy is still alive, she makes it clear that he has to work hard to become a real boy. In sharp contrast to his response to the Cricket, Pinocchio reacts positively to her. The themes of needing to recognize one's shortcomings, feeling a sense of 'good' guilt, the experience of forgiveness, and developing a good heart are prominent here. Alas, Pinocchio's rehabilitation is far from complete. Like the back-and-forth that characterizes progressive change in treatment, Pinocchio again succumbs to old habits and, instead of attending the Fairy's party to celebrate his becoming a real boy, is led astray by a bad companion, Lampwick, to Funland—a supposed utopia devoid of school and work. His subsequent misadventures include being turned into a donkey, injured while performing in a circus, and thrown into the ocean to drown. He turns back into a puppet, is swallowed by a large shark—reminiscent of the biblical Jonah (Guroian, 1998; Gaylin, 1990; Arieti, 1975)—and discovers his father in the shark's belly. Better able to bear guilt and feel remorse, Pinocchio expresses true concern for his father, who forgives him. Pinocchio then risks his life to help his father escape—a major advance toward the 'good' guilt that leads to reparation.

Because of the son, his father has become ill, and Pinocchio tries to nurse him back to health. In therapy, I like to refer to reparation (Klein, 1937; Segal, 1974) as a 'first-aid kit in your heart.' Pinocchio's working as a donkey, turning a water wheel to earn nourishment for his sick father, is a clear image of this process, emphasizing the repetitive, time-consuming work this requires. After his father has been restored to health, Pinocchio manages to save enough money to buy himself clothes, but learning that the Fairy is ill, he gives her his money and plans to continue working to support her. Concern for others has replaced his greedy self-centeredness. In response to Pinocchio's finally developing a solid 'good heart,' the Fairy forgives him for his misdeeds and promises to complete his transformation into a real boy.

Pinocchio has undergone what Wurmser (2007) after George Eliot, refers to as 'tragic transformation,' a *"process of profound change brought about by suffering, through massive inner conflict (particularly conflicts of conscience), through insight, and through action, or active work, in behalf of somebody else or in the service of the great cause"* (p. 45, my italics). Furthermore, he considers this dynamic to be "the essential process of change in an effective psychoanalysis or psychoanalytically oriented psychotherapy" (p. 46).

THE CASE OF MARK: MUSIC AS REPARATION

My work with Mark, now 22, encapsulates the process of change so compellingly charted in Pinocchio's journey. I began seeing Mark in 5x/week psychoanalytic therapy when he was six years old. We read the Disney *Pinocchio* countless times and later watched and discussed the Begnini film (2002), before reading the Collodi original when he was in his midteens. Mark later said, "That version is much darker and more serious. Unlike the jolly, lovable Pinocchio in Disney, in the original he's a mean, spoiled, selfish puppet who causes trouble constantly, although he does eventually pay his dues and become a real boy in the end." Mark, who initially met the diagnostic criteria for Asperger's, resonated with Pinocchio's journey from imprisonment to freedom, from isolation and extreme dependence to loving connections and a competent, separate self. Mark's development of 'feelings muscles,' his hard work, determination, and use of his considerable talent have all led to his remarkable transformation.

At first, Mark was extremely shy, avoided eye contact, and would 'meow' like a cat when he met people. At home, unless things went exactly his way, he threw terrible tantrums. In the waiting room, before our initial meeting, he drew the Titanic hitting the iceberg—a vivid image of his feelings of terror and no escape. (Years later, he pointed out that he had drawn a vampire with fangs and evil eyes in the iceberg, making clear the role his destructive rage played in his troubles.) Initially, he was quite scared of me; when he reached for a toy in my office he made sure his mother's hand enclosed his. He loaded up a small table with toys and was concerned it would collapse under the enormous weight, which I understood as representing his feelings about his emotional burdens. As we were ending the first session, he clung to mother, placing the corner of her sweater in his mouth.

Now, a college student majoring in psychology and doing well academically, Mark is nearing completion of a book in which he poignantly describes his descent into Asperger's:

> "As a very young boy, I was almost always extremely shy and hated meeting new people. . . . I started to feel a desire to seclude myself into my own world. . . . I became preoccupied with . . . things relating to violence or conflict and would think of these while jumping up and down" for long periods of time. He was extremely resistant to any attempts to alter this behavior.

According to Mark: "This felt great. . . . Just escaping from the real world and . . . living in my own where I was in complete control . . . [I was] literally jumping away reality." However, his efforts to escape reality became a terrible prison.

As mentioned earlier, it's crucial for the therapist to be able to see the loving person imprisoned within the hard protective shell. A song written by Mark as a teenager describes the beginning of treatment as getting "a doctor to save me so I wouldn't have to be so scared to set my good heart free." Soon, some of Mark's truly remarkable positive qualities emerged. Six months into treatment he told his mother, "when I get older I'm going to have a normal life like you and Dad," reflecting his real optimism that with his parents' and my help, coupled with his own effort, he could change.

But despite his desire for help, Mark feared needing people. He protected himself by acting like he didn't care, trashing our work, refusing to cooperate, and retreating into his own world. A real emotional battle ensued because of his fears of vulnerability if he depended on me. Like Pinocchio, Mark rejected the help I offered. In one session, Mark asked for a cup to get some water. After drinking the water, he tore the cup into bits shouting, "You only got me water! You didn't get me food!" In his book, Mark reflects upon this incident: "What I was doing was a disguised reflection on my distaste towards the world for what . . . it had failed to give me [and] helped bring to light a major conflict in my personality . . . a resentment towards life and a strong envy for those around me who had it so much easier."

During the second year of treatment, Mark became quite attached to my hand-puppet raccoon that he had named 'Wrinkles' and decided to have a birthday party for him. He came in loaded with gifts—a handmade four-poster bed with a handmade quilt, monogrammed pajamas, along with hand-painted napkins and cupcakes—all for Wrinkles. The next day, Mark pretended to kill and eat Wrinkles, whom he served boiled, roasted over a fire, and chopped and fried. Mark agreed when I said that after killing and eating Wrinkles whom he loved so much, he felt he would have him inside forever and never lose him—a vivid illustration of omnipotent control of others to avoid the passive experience of loss.

After a few years of treatment, we played out an ongoing story with Playmobile figures. I was assigned the role of Duke, a policeman. Mark played all the other parts, including Duke's enemy, the evil Zorn. During one episode, Duke helped Zorn and they were becoming friends. Then Zorn shot Duke. Mark announced, "and for the first time Zorn felt shame"—a significant step toward 'good' conscience development. After a period of years, Duke evolved into a psychologist and a prison warden in a benevolent prison that helped criminals transform into loving people. This storyline provided many opportunities to confront issues relating to imprisonment and freedom.

Creativity has been linked to both the open system mode of self-regulation (Novick and Novick, 2001, 2003) and to reparation (Segal, 1952; Klein, 1937). At sixteen, Mark began writing songs that provide a compelling road map to his inner life and growth in treatment. I see Mark's music as a genuine form of reparation. These first songs chart the familiar movement from imprisonment to recognition of destructiveness, to helpful guilt, to reparation and finally to transformation. One of his earliest was entitled "Let Me Out"; though unfinished, the fragments are quite expressive of his experience of emotional imprisonment:

> I'm sitting on my ice cold doorstep weeping away my love.
> Thinking what's the value of this place that I call hell.
> You can't unlock my chains.
> So ice my thoughts down with fear
> As I sit in this cold dark room.

Another song, "Past and Present," accurately describes the early atmosphere of our work and his multiple forms of attack.

no doctor can stop me because I just don't care
not even with these stupid daily meetings
chorus: I'm just selfish
and just won't cooperate
I'm just a nightmare
I won't communicate
I'll just stay here inside my mind
just like a knot you can't unwind
because I don't know what will become of me

The song, "Guilty Feelings," soon followed.

I often think about all of the things that I've done
How I almost let myself down and spat on everyone
The memory burns badly and I feel so angry that
I never felt this way before.
I'll never run away again.
This is how I'm recovering after so long.
And we're moving uphill as we learn from our mistakes.

Substantial growth followed, chronicled in the song, "Growing Up," that expressed a greater sense of responsibility, individuation, and self-esteem. However, this dramatic transformation was too frightening, and the song was never completed. Within weeks, Mark's songwriting came to a screeching halt. He became withdrawn, uncommunicative, and did not fully emerge from his shell until four months later. Not surprisingly, Mark's next song was entitled, "Don't Need to Grow Up." However, in the next two years Mark made considerable progress in becoming more connected. His motivation and effort in all areas of life were increasing. Conversely, during the unstructured summer break, Mark again withdrew, became preoccupied, spent considerable time posturing in front of mirrors, and during our sessions would grimace as if experiencing an inner battle. As in Pinocchio, this pattern of growth followed by returning difficulties is extremely common and can be thought of as shifting between the open and closed systems of self-regulation. Nevertheless, during this period Mark did manage to write what he still considers one of his most important songs, entitled "Burning Motivations."

All the things that I've come so far for I'm wasting away
And it takes me, and it breaks me, but I just won't let it go
It's killing me but I don't want to stop
And I'm burning away the motivation inside

The double meaning of the title, "Burning Motivations," conveys not only strong determination but also the impulse to destroy that determination, evident in this image of a destructive conscience with its emphasis on self-punishment, self-imposed suffering, and resistance to positive growth and change.

Until 1-1/2 years ago, Mark would literally spend hours jumping by the side of the road or posturing and staring into the mirror. His song, "No Escape," describes his realization that living in his own world as a way of trying to escape from painful reality actually imprisoned him.

> *Those times I'd spend staring in the mirror*
> *and see my arms around you though there's no one there*
> *Now I know, it's no escape no more*

His music tells a story of movement—from feeling imprisoned and shut off from love to freedom and loving connections. The song, "With Me," expresses a sense of loving object constancy. Although his journey is not over, Mark has really developed a 'good heart.'

> *'cause I can feel you watchin', everytime I turn out the lights*
> *And I'm breathin,' cause I feel you with me tonight*
> *I'm just so used to seein' your same old face every day*
> *But now those times are gone and I'm afraid I can no longer stay*
> *Your voice inside my head is still guiding me towards the distant light*

CONCLUDING REMARKS

Carlo Collodi's story, *Pinocchio*, elucidates aspects of the growth-promoting process of development as well as its opposite, the route to psychological disturbance. In my chapter a primary focus has been the crucial role played by alternative forms of guilt in determining the eventual outcome. The effects of helpful guilt, which facilitates progressive, adaptive development over the course of life, have been contrasted with the repercussions of destructive guilt, which underlies psychopathology. In his journey to a 'good heart,' Pinocchio progresses from a wooden and self-centered existence to freedom and the capacity to give and receive love via a remorseful guilt and reparation. In crucial ways a patient's development over the course of a helpful analytic treatment mirrors Pinocchio's journey.

This reading of *Pinocchio* has guided my highly selective review of the psychoanalytic literature concerning developmental and clinical processes. When, as in *Pinocchio*, excessive threat and vulnerability dominate childhood experience, a growth-disturbing system of emotional self-regulation develops. Pathological defenses against sadness and need, especially hostility and omnipotence, interfere with the young child's full engagement in crucial growth-promoting developmental interactions. A vicious cycle leads to ever-increasing emotional conflicts and constriction. As with Pinocchio, a sense of imprisonment develops. In psychoanalytic treatment, the interpretation of defenses against giving and receiving love within the transference opens the patient to participation in new developmental opportunities. The experience of guilt, remorse, and reparative intent for attacks within the therapeutic relationship facilitates the development of a growth-promoting mode of self-regulation. The increasing capacity to accept loss and need as well as the operation of a helpful conscience foster an upward developmental spiral leading to love, freedom, and creativity.

Finally, Mark undergoes a remarkable transformation during psychoanalytic treatment from an isolated and excessively dependent young boy to a competent, separate, and creative individual able to engage in loving relationships. His developmental path shows striking parallels to Pinocchio's journey from imprisonment to freedom. Illustrations from his therapy, along with recent autobiographical material from Mark's book, depict his initial avoidance of emotional pain and the subsequent destructive descent into a highly restrictive, imprisoning mode of self-regulation. His transformation is also portrayed; Mark develops the ability to bear sadness and endure the necessary pain of loss along with the allied capacity to feel a helpful guilt for destructive attacks on loved ones. Mark's musical lyrics—considered a form of reparation—chart his remarkable progress. In addition, my work with Mark illustrates the potentially enormous role that fairy tales and children's stories, such as *Pinocchio*, can play in child analysis.

THREE

Conscious and *The Uncanny* in Psychoanalysis and in *Pinocchio*

Elaine Zickler, Ph.D.

Dr. Singletary reminds us that psychoanalysis is a dialogue of love. It is sustained by an assurance of devoted attention and safety and by what must already be in the possession of the analyst and analysand, in however vestigial a form: a faith in the outcome. Certainly, the journey he embarks on with Mark at age five and sustains until age twenty-two bears fruit for Mark in a greater sense of freedom, an ability to tolerate feelings that he had warded off for most of his life, and a blossoming of creativity and life-force. Dr. Singletary narrates parallel stories of Pinocchio and of his patient Mark. Drawing on the work of Melanie Klein and others on the early maternal superego, Dr. Singletary directs our attention to the inevitable intersections between moral discourse and psychoanalysis. In his interpretation, both Pinocchio and Mark travel paths that lead them from 'bad conscience' and 'bad guilt' to 'good conscience' and 'good guilt,' along the way learning by hard-won experience the difference between being a puppet and being a real boy. There is an implicit moral, even Christian, allegory proceeding from fall—Mark's 'fall' into Asperger's—to redemption in these parallel narratives of conscience and psychoanalysis.

'GOOD,' 'BAD,' AND THE SUPEREGO CONCEPT

The use of 'good' and 'bad' to describe the progress of an analysis places us in the realm of moral and theological discourse. In psychoanalysis, these words spoken by our analysands attract our attention as evidence

29

of some splitting, an intolerance of necessary ambiguities and uncertainties and a way to externalize ambivalence. When we notice our theoretical and clinical language tending toward the moralistic, it is time to reflect. Our theories of the superego, whether Freudian or Kleinian, have extended and complicated the common vernacular uses of the concept of conscience without using the language of morality in order to do so. Freud's genius was in his refusal to accept the naturalizing tendencies in language without subjecting them to rigorous analysis; Klein's use of 'good' and 'bad' with reference to the fantasied breast and penis was in the context of the infantile paranoid-schizoid position of splitting and projection. In a vernacular or theological sense, one can more easily imagine a good angel (or cricket) on one shoulder and a bad one on the other, whispering into one's ears and urging one toward good or bad actions. In a psychoanalytic sense, however, the moral question of guilt gets complicated by our knowledge of unconscious guilt and the stubborn and moralistic gratifications of sadistic and masochistic positions. Infantile sexuality and aggression are not 'bad'; in our analytic practice we bestow a benevolent gaze on them. In her "Symposium on Child-Analysis," Klein insists that only by bringing the feared drive impulses to consciousness can the early harsh superego be softened and sado-masochistic object relations be tempered by kindness and trust.

Freud takes up the concept of conscience as an inheritance of the Protestant Reformation, the 'still, small voice' of reason and divine goodness, but also as an inheritance of the nineteenth-century novel, with its multiple and relativistic moral perspectives. In psychoanalysis, the conscience is a player in a complex field of psychodynamics in a mind divided between conscious and unconscious awareness. It is not only what we have done and know we have done that is now capable of making us feel guilt, what the Medieval writers called 'the agenbite of inwit,' but in the Freudian universe, it is also what we have done in our unconscious minds that is capable of tormenting us with guilt. Furthermore, and more confusingly, we are capable of experiencing feelings of moral gratification at the severe punishments that our superegos level against our egos for these unconscious offenses and even to unconsciously seek them out. The moral theologians of the seventeenth-century had a glimmer of this state of affairs when they categorized consciences in three sorts: erring, doubting, or scrupulous (Perkins, 1966). Most people fell into the 'doubting' category and were in need of guidance or the relief of confession. Those who were scrupulous were likely inhibiting themselves from acting due to an overly punitive or scrupulous conscience and were in need of reassurance and relief from unnecessary guilt. These people suffered from a 'bad conscience' without having done anything bad. An erring conscience might come closest to what Dr. Singletary calls a 'bad conscience,' one that actively urges to doing bad things, but here is where psychoanalysis makes clear what moral theology tends to confuse. A 'bad' or erring conscience is what we psychoanalysts would think of as the urging of the drives, of the id, as Freud and Klein both agreed, reserving the role of conscience or superego to that which prohibits or censures these urges (Blass, 2012). An overly severe superego is the equivalent of a bad or scrupulous conscience as we commonly understand these terms in that it prohibits us from acting at all and will not allow us to feel good regardless of whether we have done bad things in reality. The ability to acknowledge bad deeds and feel remorse is the achievement of a mature superego, as is the ability to refrain from over-scrupulosity and from deriving moral gratification from a sadistic superego.

In our work, we are not only interpreting defenses against painful affect, we are interpreting defenses against warded-off drive derivatives, against sexual guilt from the oedipal stage and early, infantile guilt about destructive fantasies and wishes (Stone, 1994). Melanie Klein was an insistent interpreter of the Oedipus complex in her young patients, although she diverged from Freud in situating the oedipal constellation much earlier in the infant's life and conceptualized a superego that was in the first place maternal and involved with the maternal body and its fantasized contents. It was a superego that was orally sadistic, harsh, and severe. In this internal object world of fantasied parental monsters, according to Klein, this sadism is projected externally and the child "turns his objects into dangerous ones" (Klein, 1933, p. 250). In this way, the relation between the id and the superego, which Freud had already explained as one of inheritance, the superego deriving its prohibitive force from the strength of the aggressive and sexual wishes of the id, is again elaborated as a kind of mirror image, a projected return of the violence of internal impulses in the form of a harsh, prohibitive, and punitive conscience. This early superego is immature and harsh; Freud's oedipal instantiation of the superego is comprised of a more mature and loving aspect, reflecting a psyche, theoretically speaking, that has had to renounce the omnipotence of infancy and the all-or-nothing narcissism of the phallic stage in return for a more reasonable and forgiving stance toward self and others. This superego now stands in for the loving father, the father of protection and security, the source of the 'oceanic feeling' described by his friend, Romain Rolland (Freud, 1930). This 'father of pre-history' (Kristeva, 1996) and its avatar in the form of the superego, is the guarantor of the child's place in the symbolic order and as such encompasses family, country, culture, and religion—all those stabilizing and idealized elements that give us our identities and make us want to live up to them.

In our theoretical language and assumptions we have to guard against confusing our psychoanalytic goals of treatment with what might be the goals of social adaptation and conformity to community or cultural norms. Pinocchio, in Collodi's tale, in fact never expresses the wish to be a real boy. Geppetto bemoans the fact that he is not acting like a 'respectable puppet'; the Blue Fairy tells him that he must 'accustom [himself] to being a respectable boy'; and, at the very end, when Pinocchio is changed into a real boy and looks at himself in the mirror, he sees himself as a 'respectable boy.' Because Dr. Singletary's use of the language of 'good' and 'bad' is part of a general drift in our psychoanalytic literature, it would be worthwhile to address the question of the intersection of the moral and the psychoanalytic discourses in theory and in clinical practice.

PINOCCHIO, MARK, AND FREUD'S 'UNCANNY'

Having posed this question for consideration, I am going to offer a different psychoanalytic reading of *Pinocchio,* making use of Freud's essay, *The Uncanny*, and drawing from Dr. Singletary's case material from Mark's analysis. In *The Uncanny,* Freud analyzed the specific ways in which the uncanny affects us and categorized them as: the threat of castration; the double or *doppelganger,* including the role of the mirror-double; and the compulsion to repeat. Here, in this descending order of development, we see the oedipal stage threat of castration; the mirror-stage threat of the other, as well as the estrangement of the self-image in the first moment of primary narcissism; and, the compulsion to repeat, linked with the maternal body and genitals and the threats they pose to the emerging ego. Freud characterizes the uncanny in the German terms, *heimlich* and *unheimlich,* or homely and unhomely, antithetical terms which tend to merge in the unconscious. What is most strange or uncanny turns out upon analysis to be most familiar or close to home because what is homely has become unhomely, or strange, by way of repression. (This is a familiar trope in many works of literature, specifically in children's literature; we might think of *The Wizard of Oz* or *Alice in Wonderland*.) As a point of origin, Freud situates the homeliest place in the genitals and womb of the mother, universally forgotten or repressed and returning in experiences of the uncanny (Freud, 1919, p. 245). Let us consider these three uncanny moments as they emerge and interact in *Pinocchio* and in Mark's analysis and song lyrics.

The compulsion to repeat, manifested in Pinocchio's repetitious behaviors and in Mark's repetitive jumping and withdrawing, can be thought of as stubborn naughtiness, as refusal to remain 'in reality,' as Mark writes about himself. If we think about this compulsion as linked to the demonic quality of the death drive and also to the threat posed by the return to the body of the mother, we have a different take on this 'bad'-ness. Pinocchio begins life enclosed in a large piece of wood. Like Oedipus, he seems to lack a primal scene. His efforts to escape his origins result, as with Oedipus, in an ironic return to them. His life becomes a series of near-death experiences until the very last episode where he enters the toothy mouth of a huge shark and finds there, world within world, a swallowed ship and Geppetto again. This is the mother's biting vagina and her womb, into which he enters, descends, and nearly dies before his determined escape. He is a bundle of drives and urges, of untrammeled energy. From the moment Geppetto fashions him into a puppet and projects onto him his own fantasy that he should become a real boy, Pinocchio is awash in ambivalence, trying to gratify his own needs, feeling guilty about his greed and deficiencies. Above all, he is hungry, starving, screaming, and crying, an orally sadistic infant whose every wish for gratification brings on a violent punishment all out of proportion to what he's done. We see quite graphically the overwhelming power of his infantile drives and their projected return as harsh punishments. He has a good heart, but is mistreated by others who abuse his childish narcissism and naiveté.

Consider the episode where Pinocchio runs out into a stormy night to look for food. Geppetto has been taken to jail for trying to beat Pinocchio in the street; he is described as a brutal 'tyrant' and he has failed to carve ears for his puppet! Pinocchio has, indeed, killed the cricket who calls him a 'bad boy' and finds himself in a house where there is only a simulacrum of food—images painted on the walls of fruit and a kettle. He goes out and begs for food from a 'respectable old man' who thinks he is a 'young tough' and who responds to his pleas by dumping a bucket of water on his head from a second story window. Pinocchio goes home, drenched, still starving, falls asleep by the brazier and burns off his feet!

Now, recall the moment when Mark, as a young boy, asked Dr. Singletary for water and then complained angrily that "it wasn't food." What strikes one is that what is being defended against by Mark's complaint against Dr. Singletary and by Pinocchio's two terrible punishments for hunger and childishness is the desire for more, greedy, yes, but also quite sexual, even if completely out of awareness and disguised. Perhaps Mark, as Dr. Singletary maintains, was defending against gratitude and fighting dependency by expressing ingratitude; it makes sense. But perhaps he was also complaining that he never gets what he really wants and though he can't say what it is, it's really much, much more than a glass of water. He wants real food and he wants it from Dr. Singletary; Pinocchio, too, wants real food, not a painted image on the wall. His desires take on a decided oedipal cast when he burns off his feet by way of punishment, moreover. The sexual, as Klein insisted, was there early on in the child, as was the horror of bodily disintegration, a proto-castration. Was Mark trying to hurt his feet or destroy them by repeated jumping? Or, again, in the lyrics to "Burning Motivations," is he alluding to Pinocchio's burned-off feet, to his own frustrated, forbidden incestuous desires, when he repeats that he is 'All stuck down below' and that he is 'burning away the motivation inside'? One has to be curious about Mark's sexuality during those long years of analysis, from pre-latency through to young adulthood, especially in light of the erotic and romantic longing of his song lyrics. How did it manifest itself in the transference with Dr. Singletary? In what occulted ways did he express his desires, his guilt, and his self-punishment?

A BRIEF FORAY INTO WINNICOTT AND LACAN

Mirror images and doubles figure in both *Pinocchio* and in Mark's analysis and song writing. There are two key texts on the role of the mirror stage in development: Lacan's and Winnicott's. Both of these can be read with reference to Freud's essay on *The Uncanny*. Lacan's mirror phase posits a pre-verbal and pre-ambulatory child held up in front of a mirror. The child becomes fascinated with its own image in what Lacan considers a uniquely human fashion. For Lacan, this mirror image inaugurates the birth of the ego in a spatially and temporally divided sense of itself. The infant sees an image that is enticing and that seduces her into the future, into an illusory 'ego ideal.' Henceforth, she will never feel completely at one with herself, but will always be haunted by the seduction of the mirror image. The image presents the child with a formal unity that is lacking in the child's own experience of its body which is in need of external support, typically by the mother. The fascination with this image is already underlined or haunted by a kind of horror or fear of disintegration, thereafter defended against by both externalization and internalization, by projection and introjection (Lacan, 1949; Klein, 1933).

Winnicott reads Lacan's paper and produces his own, quite characteristic version of the mirror phase in which the child sees himself reflected in his mother's gaze, benign, malign, or indifferent (Winnicott, 1971). In Lacan's version, the mirror mediates the dyadic reality; in Winnicott's version, there is no mediating mirror, only the dyadic fascination of the two faces, mother and child. For Lacan, the mirror image produces an inevitable non-correspondence between self and image; for Winnicott, it is a primary catastrophe when the mother's gaze doesn't conform to the child's sense of itself. For Lacan, this non-correspondence inaugurates the divided ego and primary narcissism. Following on Freud, Klein, Lacan, and Laplanche, primary narcissism refers to the earliest phase of subject-object differentiation and not to a stage of un-differentiation as in Mahler's 'autistic' or 'symbiotic' stage. Implicitly, narcissism makes reference to this split and to the possibility of reflecting on an image of oneself as object, a 'mirror-type relation.' "There seems to be no reason why 'primary narcissism' should not designate an early phase or formative moments, marked by the emergence of a first adumbration of the ego and its immediate libidinal cathexis. This is not to say that this first narcissism represents the earliest state of the human being, nor, economically speaking, that such a predominance of self-love rules out any object-cathexis"

(Laplanche and Pontalis, 1973, p. 338). This primary narcissism inaugurates the ego in these theories. As with Mahler, there is an ongoing process of differentiation and individuation from this point on. There is no
sense, as in Winnicott, however, of a falling away from dyadic wholeness
that is in need of repair. These are significant theoretical divergences and
lead, inexorably, to different kinds of discourses. Our developmental literature has, in the main, chosen Winnicott's mirror over Lacan's, so it is
worth considering what Lacan's model offers that Winnicott's seems to
elide.

The mirror stage provides both a developmental and an erotogenic
ideal and motivation in Lacan's theory while unleashing a sense of alienation with its accompanying aggression and narcissism. The fascination,
so characteristic of the maternal transference, is an experience of awe as
well as envy, of idealization and almost unbearable self-erasure. If we
look at Lacan's and Winnicott's accounts through the later theorizing of
Laplanche on the 'implantation' of sexuality in the infant by way of the
mother's 'enigmatic' (because unconscious to her) sexual messages, we
can be more specific about the mediation of the third, or other, into this
version of the mirror, one that is quite absent in Winnicott's account, for
whom the mother is only able to be need-satisfying or not and without
any unconscious sexuality of her own which might color her gaze at, or
nurturing of, her infant. The root of 'fascination' is in bewitchment, so
that gazing into the mirror of the mother's face carries with it an aura of
enchantment that partakes not only of mutual recognition and exchange
of loving glances, but also of inchoate erotic yearning, dependence, captivity, and alienation. Recall Mark's memory of being a baby in the strol-
ler and avoiding the gaze of others; Pinocchio, in translation, is "wooden,
or pine, eyes" among other possible meanings, suggesting an intense
anxiety about seeing and being seen in return.

The gap in subjectivity introduced by Lacan's mirror phase is a proto-
type of castration anxiety and later oedipal anxieties evoked by the spec-
ter of object loss and narcissistic insufficiency. Neil Hertz (1985), writing
about Laplanche and anxiety formulates "a litany of nervous questions . . . that give expression to epistemological anxiety (can I trust my
eyes?), to narcissism (can I hold myself together?), to sexual anxiety (can I
hold on to my penis?), to—beyond that—social and economic fears about
property and status (can I hold onto anything, including representations
of myself?)" (p. 204). Pinocchio embodies and represents these primal
anxieties in his repetitive experiences of loss and of his inability to hold
onto anything—his nose, his schoolbook, his money, even his own best
intentions. Dr. Singletary's patient, Mark, in his songs repeats refrains
that express on the one side, the omnipotent infantile fantasy of "a time
when I could reach out and just take it all" and on the other, the horror of
losing, as in the nightmare scenario of "Last Night" where even his fantasies must be lost: "All the stories that you wrote, they're all gone."

In Freud's *The Uncanny*, the mirror functions as a saboteur of the self. Before one recognizes oneself in the mirror, there is first a moment of decided unease and non-recognition. In an extended footnote to the essay, Freud relates the uncanny mirror experiences of the writer Ernst Mach and then of his own similar experience while riding in a train compartment. A violent jolt of the train caused the door of a washing cabinet to swing open and Freud assumed that a strange man had walked into his compartment by mistake. "Jumping up with the intention of putting him right, I at once realized to my dismay that the intruder was nothing but my own reflection in the looking-glass on the open door. I can still recollect that I thoroughly disliked his appearance. Instead, therefore, of being frightened by our 'doubles,' both Mach and I simply failed to recognize them as such. Is it not possible, though, that our dislike of them was a vestigial trace of the archaic reaction which feels the 'double' to be something uncanny?" (Freud, 1919, fn. p. 248). The mirror doubles the self in an experience of the uncanny and this experience Freud theorizes as the prototypical experience of the observing ego, of the 'passing of primary narcissism,' and a precursor to the super ego: "The fact that an agency of this kind exists, which is able to treat the rest of the ego like an object—the fact, that is, that man is capable of self-observation—renders it possible to invest the old idea of a 'double' with a new meaning and to ascribe a number of things to it—above all, those things which seem to self-criticism to belong to the old surmounted narcissism of earliest times" (Freud, 1919, p. 235). Freud notes the difficult distinction that he would draw between this observing function, the 'splitting of the ego,' and the split in the ego between the conscious and unconscious parts. It is difficult to draw this distinction because what is repressed and unconscious is also what is disavowed and rejected by the ego.

BACK TO PINOCCHIO AND MARK

Consider the episode in *Pinocchio* where both he and Lampwick have been transformed into jackasses. Pinocchio first feels the changes in his body, the lengthening of his ears, and goes in "search of a mirror so that he could look at himself, but since he couldn't find a mirror, he filled the hand basin with water and, looking at his reflection in it, saw what he never would have wished to see: he saw, that is, his own image embellished by a magnificent pair of asinine ears. . . . He began to cry, to shriek, to bang his head on the wall, but the more he despaired, the more his ears grew, and grew, and grew, and became hairy toward the tips" (Collodi, 1991, p. 165). Soon after, he goes in search of Lampwick, who has also begun an identical transformation into a jackass. Pinocchio, in order to mask his transformation, first puts a big cotton cap on his head and pulls it down over his face. He knocks on Lampwick's door and after a long delay, Lampwick opens with a big cotton cap on his head as well. Here is another mirror-image, this time with Lampwick as his double. The two of them feign belief in each other's lies about the reason for the cotton caps, then fall into "a very long silence, during which the two friends did nothing but look at each other mockingly"(Collodi, 1991, p. 168). They then work up to mutual uncapping and, "instead of being mortified and afflicted"(p. 169), they burst into loud laughter. Here, the sight of the externalized *doppelganger* invokes ridicule and laughter as if in denial of the affliction that each of them suffers in their own transformed images. Or, more disturbingly, it depicts the failure of the dyadic gaze to mediate the aggression and sadism unleashed by this mirroring.

There are two distinct mirror-moments represented in this scene: non-recognition of the self, as when Pinocchio looks at his own reflection and sees his donkey ears; and the self as a foreign other on whom one can project sadistic feelings and ridicule, as when Pinocchio and Lampwick ridicule each other's 'jack-ass-ness.' At the end of the story, there will be yet another mirror-image of this moment of mortification when Pinocchio again wakes up only to discover that he has been changed into a real boy. Again, he goes to the mirror "and he looked like someone else. He no longer saw the usual image of the wooden marionette reflected there, but he saw the lively and intelligent image of a handsome young lad with brown hair, blue eyes, and as happy and gay an air as if he were in heaven" (Collodi, 1991, p. 207). This is the third mirror-moment of primary narcissistic love.

Julia Kristeva (1982) offers the notion of 'abjection' to account for an intermediate defensive process prior to the formation of the mature superego. This zone of abjection has many affinities with Freud's uncanny, coming into play "on the fragile border . . . where identities (subject/object, etc.) do not exist or only barely so" (p. 207). For Kristeva, this first 'splitting of the ego' results not yet in repression, but in a "massive and sudden emergence of uncanniness, . . . [that] harries me as radically separate, loathsome. Not me. Not that. But not nothing, either. A weight of meaninglessness, about which there is nothing insignificant. . . . On the edge of non-existence and hallucination, of a reality that, if I acknowledge it, annihilates me. There, abject and abjection are my safeguards" (p. 2). In the category of what must be 'abjected,' thinking of Mark, we might place dependency on the mother, as well as all those pre-genital drive derivatives; aggressive, devouring, and destructive wishes against the mother; and the reciprocal fears of the mother that co-exist with these wishes. With some poignancy, Pinocchio asks of a large fish, "Would you do me the favor of telling me if there are any towns on this island where one can eat without running the risk of being eaten?" (Collodi, 1991, p. 113). Like Pinocchio, Mark is "devouring and threatened with devouring" (Gross, 2011, p. 104) unless he repeatedly jumps away from threatening dependencies and threatening wishes. Like Pinocchio, Mark's repetitious jumping renders him uncanny and automaton-like. Mark repeats a refrain in his songs about not having to breathe:

> *Why I sat down and watched life drive by*
> *To breathe like the rest, as if I never had to before*
> *Those times I'd spend staring in the mirror;*

And again:

> *Fantasy, the prison where I feel free*
> *Holding back from where I would have to breathe.*

This odd locution encompasses both a wish to die and a narcissistic wish to be able to exist without dependence on breath, like a puppet or automaton. Mark rejects the 'environmental mother' in his narcissistic rage to be self-sufficient, perhaps even self-generating. In Collodi's tale, the Blue Fairy claims to be already dead when Pinocchio meets her and seems to die again when Pinocchio runs away from her. She draws Pinocchio repeatedly into situations that threaten his life and test his resolve and she is there to revive him and nurture him as well. Mark writes of seeing in his mirror his arms around someone who isn't there. This is the mother of ambivalence, the archaic mother of Kleinian and Kristevan theory, the mother consigned by Freud to the Minoan-Mycenaean era of pre-history.[1]

CONCLUDING REMARKS

Finally, we must take note of the clinical situation in which the sense of the uncanny emerges as an opening onto insight and self-reflection: a moment of inter-subjectivity as well as intra-subjectivity, where the past and the repressed emerge in the transference. The feeling of the compulsive and repetitive symptom is a feeling of the uncanny; the interpretation in the transference or the bestowal of symbolic recognition and benevolence onto the symptom has the effect of producing the uncanny feeling in the inter-subjective field, a shift from the haunting effect of its repetition to its emergence as an object of symbolic and verbal exchange. That is, both the past and the repressed or disavowed produce an effect of the uncanny when they emerge in analysis.

What is it that Pinocchio experiences at the end of the tale? When the Blue Fairy bestows flesh and blood on him, he looks at his old puppet self and says, "How funny I was when I was a puppet! And how happy I am now that I've become a respectable boy." He is narcissistically in love with his new image in the mirror and ashamed of the puppet he used to be. He is estranged from his old wooden self, but he is not yet humbled by the inevitable return of this repressed. Pinocchio, at the end of the tale, is not transformed but split into an observing and critical ego, or superego, and emerging as a subject of the unconscious. The wooden puppet cast aside into the corner remains as his uncanny double, the emblem of the alien quality of the unconscious, whether repressed or abjected, that can return at any time. It is what makes us, in Kristeva's words, "strangers to ourselves." The guilt that remains is an epistemological guilt that carries an ethical imperative. In acknowledging that we and others are more unconscious than conscious most of the time, we acknowledge that we are not fully present to our actions while being fully responsible for their consequences. We are condemned to a kind of 'afterwardsness' in Laplanche's terms (Laplanche, 1999, p. 260-267), the recipients of and translators of 'enigmatic messages' of sexual desire, passed on to us by adults in our infancy, and are responsible for trying to know why we do what we do. We are engaged simultaneously in looking backward at this enigmatic, infantile past and forward toward our narcissistic ideals and, unlike Pinocchio, are tasked with owning that wooden puppet, that impulsive doppelganger, and not simply tossing him into the corner and moving on. It is only a benign view of the infantile drives which can promote a tolerant view of that wooden double instead of a continuation of dejection, abjection, and projection as modes of relating to the self and to others.

NOTE

1. The connection between the maternal and the death drive is clearly on Freud's mind at this time. In this same year, 1919, he is writing *Beyond the Pleasure Principle*, where both the death drive and the repetition compulsion are theorized at length. The maternal is the missing link, as it were. In *The Uncanny*, the bedrock of repression, what generates the uncanny sense of repetition is ultimately the mother's body; in *Beyond the Pleasure Principle*, the compulsion to repeat is linked to the death drive.

FOUR

Bearable and Unbearable Guilt: A Kleinian Perspective

Desy Safán-Gerard, Ph.D.

The purpose of this paper is to present detailed material from four analytic sessions with a patient who seemed unable, until the last session, to bear guilt. The material of the first two sessions illustrates in detail the vicissitudes of guilt, how the patient comes into contact with it and then avoids it employing various defenses. The last two sessions reveal the consequences of the work of the two earlier sessions. Based on this clinical material, I question interpretations that address defenses against guilt but fail to help the patient bear the guilt. When the patient cannot bear the guilt, attempts other than reparation are resorted to that tend to arrest development and produce a regressive movement in the analysis. The sessions show how the analyst's interpretations of the patient's evasions and other defenses against guilt can make the analyst prey to a sadomasochistic enactment in the transference whereby the patient expiates the guilt and reverts to a lack of recognition of what he or she does to his or her objects. The analyst's concern with the patient's defenses against the emergence of conscious guilt needs to be balanced by equal attention to the patient's incipient experience of guilt and the loving feelings embodied in this guilt. The bearability of guilt is increased both by a diminution of the patient's destructiveness and by the mobilization of love, which helps mitigate such destructiveness.

The experience of conscious guilt represents a key moment in an analysis. Love and hate have finally come together and love begins to surmount hatred. If patients can bear the guilt, they take responsibility for their neglect and/or sadistic attacks on their objects and move toward reparation. Both Freud (1930) and Klein (1935, 1940, 1948) conceive of guilt as due to aggressive impulses toward the object. However, Klein adds a new dimension to Freud's notion of unconscious guilt as a search for punishment. Guilt becomes the driving force of depressive anxiety (resulting from prior hostile attacks on the loved object) and manifests in the consulting room as conscious guilt. Within the Kleinian framework, guilt is a 'marker' of development, in that it typically initiates reparative efforts toward the external as well as the internal object. The person may attempt to restore the object or manically defend against an acknowledgment of his or her attacks on it. When guilt is short-circuited in this defensive way, it remains unconscious with various consequences. If, for example, in the analytic situation, the hostility and guilt toward the object is projected onto the analyst, the patient becomes a victim of the sadism perceived in the analyst. This can lead to a sado-masochistic enactment in the transference in which the analyst's countertransference plays an important part.

How we understand guilt's unbearability will determine the stance we take with our patients. If we believe that guilt results from an unrealistically harsh superego, our aim will be to help the patient free himself or herself from this excessively demanding superego; if we believe that guilt is a necessary response to an awareness of the individual's own destructiveness, our goal will be to help the patient bear the guilt so that reparation for the fantasized or real attacks on his or her objects can take place. The analyst who is helping the patient to become aware of his or her guilt might be seen as colluding with the patient's harsh superego by becoming an external superego figure. This would trap the patient into a masochistic submission to his or her harsh superego. From a Kleinian perspective, on the other hand, an analyst who, in an attempt to help free the patient from excessive guilt, interprets the patient's expressions of guilt as being *merely* the result of the patient's harsh superego, is bypassing an opportunity to help the patient experience guilt, restore his or her objects, and thus replace the internal damaged object with a reconstituted one. The experience of guilt may lead one to feel 'besieged' and have a wish to get rid of the guilt. But this experience of guilt does not result in persecution by an 'other,' a search for punishment or expiation, but is associated with loving feelings for the object and reparative impulses. It is interesting to note that in her later writings, Klein (1960) extended the notion of guilt as an expression of a concern for the object to include a concern for the self, that is, guilt feelings that can arise out of the awareness of having neglected and abandoned parts of one's own personality.

When we attempt to understand the immature coping responses to guilt, we enter into the complicated area of sado-masochistic relationships, how these come into play in the transference, and the kind of impasses that result from them. Also related are the complex constellations of anxieties and defenses that have come to be called narcissistic object relationships (Rosenfeld, 1964, 1971), defensive organizations (O'Shaughnessey, 1981), or pathological organizations (Steiner, 1987). Sado-masochistic enactments in the transference can be understood as projections of sadistic impulses onto the analyst while the patient becomes the analyst's victim, which, in turn, expiates the patient's guilt. In projecting sadistic impulses, the patient is also projecting the guilt connected with these impulses. By counterprojective identification the analyst may find himself or herself offering punishing or condemning interpretations *and* feeling guilty about them. Impasses created by the patient's unbearable guilt are also induced when the analyst acts out his or her *own* hatred toward the patient as a frustrating object and is then beset with his or her *own* unconscious guilt which can lead to a masochistic surrender to the patient's attacks. The patient's projected sadism into the analyst then finds an appropriate target and the analyst cannot interpret effectively in response to the patient's accusations. The analyst is then confused as to whose sadism and whose guilt are at play. Transference and countertransference feelings become entangled, underscoring the view of the analytic enterprise as a two-way street, especially at times when the analyst has lost his or her position of technical neutrality.

Steiner (1990) writes about a patient's inability to tolerate guilt which led to impasses and the eventual interruption of treatment. Steiner's patient would shift from a seductive mistreatment of friends and employees to feeling imprisoned and persecuted in the transference. The persecuted feeling represented one form of paranoid defense against guilt. Steiner explains, "just when he seemed more in contact with me, the situation would suddenly go terribly wrong, *perhaps because the guilt was unbearable* and we ended up in a confrontation where he felt criticized and attacked. He would then feel justified and I was supposed to feel guilty" (p. 90, my italics). The patient's accusations of cruelty result from projecting his or her sadism and guilt into the analyst, leading to confusion and guilt in the countertransference. Of his patient Steiner notes, "Because he (the patient) also tended to project that part of him capable of proper judgment, it was difficult for me to know whether I was interpreting *responsibly or sadistically* so that doubt and guilt threatened to undermine my judgment" (p. 90, italics mine). The patient's guilt had become Steiner's guilt, but was it only the patient's guilt?

Referring to her own countertransference regarding a patient's potential suicide, Riesenberg (1981) concludes, "This fear in the analyst, conscious and unconscious, creates a state of anxiety closely linked with guilt, which I think in turn is *stimulated and increased* by the patient's projective identifications" (p. 568, my italics). She seems to be acknowledging the role of the analyst's own guilt toward the patient, just as Steiner acknowledged his own confusion and guilt toward his patient. This guilt, which is not merely a response to the patient's projections, is probably due to damaged, unrepaired objects in the analyst's internal world and the wish to repair them in the patient or in the patient's objects (Racker, 1968). The patient's accusations arouse the analyst's guilt for his or her own neglect, abuse, or attacks on his or her objects. This may also account for the difficulties the analyst may experience in helping patients bear their guilt. Reisenberg eventually took the risk of terminating the analysis of this patient because she, as Steiner with his patient, felt unable to help him bear his guilt.

At this point, we must consider the question as to why guilt feelings are so unbearable. Guilt implies a recognition of having attacked or damaged the loved object and an acknowledgment that the attack is due to the person's own hatred. This may have been the result of envy, jealousy, or a retaliatory attack. Perhaps such recognition leads to an unconscious linking between this attack and similar attacks—conscious and unconscious—on other objects in the past. Instances of real attacks may thus link up with omnipotent unconscious attacks on the primary object and its fantasized devastating effects. Guilt then becomes unbearable because it cannot be easily assuaged through reparation since one would have to repair *all* the damage, real and fantasized. Often the pressure to quickly get past guilt leads to omnipotent, manic reparation (Rey, 1986; Segal, 1981). Because of the force of these attacks which add to the guilt's unbearability, we need to help the patient keep in mind the basic underlying love for these objects. In helping patients bear the guilt, the analyst may need to point out to them that guilt is the *evidence* of this love, without losing sight of the attacks on the objects. We need to keep in mind that a denial of guilt may be caused by unconscious envy or jealousy and the patient's reluctance to make that conscious as the cause of his or her unconscious attacks. In the case presented here one can see the connection between envious or jealous attacks and guilt. For it is the acknowledged envious or jealous attack that allows guilt to be experienced. Thus we may be dealing here with an inability to consciously experience love or with a deeply rooted destructiveness, both of which precluding the possibility of experiencing guilt.

Another way of looking at guilt's unbearability is that perhaps the patient cannot acknowledge guilt precisely because of the intrinsic connection between guilt and love toward the object. The awareness of such love makes the patient acutely aware of his or her separateness and infantile dependence on the object that he or she is manically trying to deny. Such dependency may not only arouse hatred but puts the patient in touch with his or her absent mother who threatens his or her sense of autonomy. The patient then assumes a pseudo-psychopathic stance in which he or she defends a wish not to care at all about his or her objects. The patient does that by evading, denying, and projecting guilt. This would imply that attempts by the analyst to help the patient become aware of guilt are doomed to failure because they threaten the patient's acknowledgment of infantile dependency. Taking this position argues that the primary task at hand is to bring to the patient's attention his or her reluctance to admit to loving, with the resulting anxiety of depending on an object and the fear of losing a hard-won autonomy. In light of this, it is the analyst who might have to bear the patient's psychopathic stance by not addressing the patient's defenses against guilt—denial, evasions, projection—but linking guilt with love for the object and addressing the patient's anxieties about loving and depending on an object. Some critical aspects of guilt's bearability will be illustrated in the material below where the patient is projecting guilt onto me and experiencing persecution rather than guilt.

A CLINICAL ILLUSTRATION

I will now turn to a week of sessions with David, a professional who came to me complaining about his indecisiveness in getting a divorce from his wife of twenty years from whom he had been separated for two years. He expressed considerable guilt about having left his wife, a successful professional in her own right, and their three teenage children, without warning, to pursue one of his numerous affairs. He had had affairs throughout the marriage which he considered to be with his wife's implicit approval. When he came for treatment, his independent practice had practically collapsed, together with the breakup of his family.

David was raised in a foreign country and came here escaping a fascist government. He was the oldest and only male child in his family. His father is a successful businessman and his mother is a professional. He claims to have been ill-treated by his father during his childhood. His mother, being a busy physician, was mostly unaware of the patient's emotional abuse by his father. A maid, whom he remembers fondly, played the role of mother and protected him from his father. At present, he seldom talks about his mother and still experiences intense envy of the father's success and, except for money, David either rejects or devalues the help his father offers him.

David is in his third year of analysis. During the time I have been seeing him, his promiscuity has been center stage. At the beginning of the treatment, he was involved with two or three women simultaneously, and we spent time analyzing his anxiety about depending on a single object. The most striking aspect of the treatment has been his tendency to intellectualize and his constantly showing off with his analytical sophistication as another 'conquest.' At the beginning, he seemed to want me only as a witness to his expertise and accepted my interpretations only if they supported his own. He seemed hardly aware of my presence as a partner in an exchange. My main task early on was to try to help him stay connected with his experience, rather than with his theories about his experience. The patient is still extremely skilled at evading his emotions with intellectualizations and, as he himself puts it, 'diluting' whatever is difficult to bear. David's glib responses at times create an uncomfortable feeling of an 'as—if' analysis where nothing alive is happening. He often complains at the beginning of a session that he is on 'automatic pilot' and disconnected from his real feelings. On the other hand, he can be extremely charming and has a very active social life.

David vividly describes his conflict about women. He sees women at the center and men around them as boys. In a series of relationships since his separation, he has been partially supported by his lovers, most of them older than himself. Talking once about having flirted with the wife of a good client, he says he gets excited at the idea of the 'other' desiring him but then is in turmoil because he fears his life is on the verge of disaster. It would seem that when he is desired, it excites his impulse to triumph over the woman and over the man, spoiling both the man's generosity and the woman's good feelings toward him. This seems to constitute an attack on the parental couple, a response to a primitive oedipal constellation where mommy and daddy are felt to be enjoying each other and abandoning him. With destroyed internal parents, he feels on the verge of disaster.

In spite of a reduced fee, David has been accumulating a debt to me for several months due to the current recession's effect on his profession. At present, he lives with a girlfriend, also a successful professional, toward whom he is quite ambivalent. He has been monogamous for the last year but the wish to go after other women is still present.

Monday Session

He starts the session claiming that he is tired of talking about himself. Has had several dreams but cannot remember any of them. Then he says Alma, his girlfriend, has been complaining that he is not interested in buying anything for the house. She is jealous of his previous life where he bought things. They had gone to help Alma's friend buy furniture for her computer. Alma was complaining that they do things to help a friend but not for themselves.

Here David shows once again how he is not interested in becoming a couple with his girlfriend. He also seems to be telling me he is not interested in becoming an analytic couple with me. He projects his own neediness in Alma's friend and becomes the helper.

David continues, "My internal agenda was that she would conclude that we are incompatible." This reminded him of a story he had read a couple of nights ago. "This adolescent was picked up by an older woman, a bit like what used to happen to me when I was young. . . . In the story the woman found a job for the guy. The guy gets involved in politics and finds opportunities with other women . . . The woman then throws a party and invites her fiancé. The guy manages to get her into bed so that her fiancé finds them in bed. Then the guy escapes through the window." After a short silence David says, "I just connected the story with the situation with Alma. I was thinking of telling her, 'Do you realize that I need to build my life alone, to generate an interest for my own house, for me?' This is a 'story' I have used many times in order to leave a relationship. It's a manipulation that implies that I'm too defective to be with a woman."

David's internal agenda is that she will leave him so that he doesn't have to feel guilty for abandoning her. He often talks about how generous she is with him. That troubles him because, being envious of the girlfriend's achievement, it is hard for him to experience gratitude toward her. The woman in the story helps the guy, like I help him. The guy in the story not only uses the woman but betrays her with other women, and breaks the relationship to her fiancé. He is triumphing over the envied mother in the woman because she has what he needs and she has helped him, which he resents out of envy. By this time, I am increasingly annoyed at his 'story,' at how he uses Alma, at how he uses me in the transference. The defective 'story' reflects his unwillingness to give anything to Alma, his mother, me. His manipulation and his avoidance of responsibility about how he treats his objects are clear: if he is defective, he is not accountable. I interpret how the adolescent in the story, himself, gets rid of the woman once he has used her. Wonder if it is not what he is doing with me, tired of talking about himself, unable to remember his dreams. Just as he feels with Alma, he certainly does not want to contribute anything to *our* partnership. I add that perhaps, he has the fantasy that if I believe he is too defective, I will liberate him from his analysis and he won't have to assume responsibility for having interrupted. He has talked about interrupting his analysis for a while until his financial situation improves. On the other hand, he tells me he doesn't open the envelope with his bill because he doesn't want to know how much he owes me. I believe he avoids an awareness of how he is using me, an awareness which would make his unconscious guilt, which I believe is considerable, conscious. I continue to interpret that the 'story' he told Alma about the need to use his own motivation applies to his analysis as well. He believes he has all the answers, doesn't need anything from me, and therefore there is no need to acknowledge what he is getting from women and is not grateful for what he is given. "If I interrupt your analysis, you then could say, 'She doesn't care' and then justify your not caring about being fair to me. You don't have to feel bad for using me."

David seems taken aback. He sighs and says: "Actually with Alma, I feel less guilt because I have given her more than I have given you. . . . I was asking myself if this was not directed at Vicky [*his ex-wife*]. She is older than me. It's incredible because the guilt I feel toward her, I can't feel with anybody else. Invariably, when I think about pain I think of the pain I caused her . . . " At this moment he seems to be experiencing guilt.

But this doesn't last when he adds, "Although it's different. I don't feel I have used her in the context of our relationship." We see here an incipient guilt and its denial.

David continues, "It connects me to what Alma was saying and of her jealousy of that relationship: the kids, the house . . . I was going to say that that was another stage in my life, but I didn't say that. What Alma told me made me feel pain . . . pain that I am not willing to give myself things, to fight to get a better income. We were driving in the car and I felt very hurt."

I believe the pain and hurt are not related to guilt and a concern with Alma or with me but guilt connected with his own well-being. There seems to be some guilt and concern about not hurting Alma in his refraining from saying that that was another stage in his life. However, by feeling very hurt because he doesn't give himself things he seems to be expiating this guilt. I also wonder if his not fighting to get a better income is an expression of his unconscious guilt that expresses itself in a search for punishment. I feel that something has gotten derailed after David expresses his guilt about his ex-wife. At that moment, he was in contact with this guilt. I was taken aback by the derailment and my own disappointment that interfered with my capacity to interpret. I could have brought him back to his statement about Vicky and interpreted how painful it must be for him to stay with that experience. I could have reminded him of the love he must feel toward Vicky, which explains why he feels so guilty. This might have helped him with bearing the guilt.

David now adds, "Even though there is one part of me that uses, who used Alma, who uses you, *I don't want to be a witness to all this.* Also, I was hurt that that job I was going to get, the guy canceled it. Another potential job that went to hell."

Incipient guilt again but here he spells out his unwillingness to be a witness to what he is doing to his objects. I no longer feel irritated at his manipulations and evasions as matters seem to be on the table. However, he immediately expiates the guilt by experiencing the hurt over the disappointment about the job that didn't pan out. I caught myself thinking that not willing to give himself things may be the result of projective identification. I then interpreted that whenever he might succeed at something, he puts the little David who steals, who uses others into me and then he gets anxious that I am going to take advantage of him and use him. Maybe this anxiety of me robbing him makes him lose his motivation to make more money. While concentrating in the way he expiates guilt, I missed stressing how very painful it is to be a witness to all this, especially because he also cares a great deal about Alma and about me. The notion that his painful guilt is connected to love might have helped him bear his guilt. I continue to elaborate his fear of being robbed, providing him with some evidence. I remind him that sometimes when he tells me that something at work went well, he immediately adds that it was just a *little* job. I add, "Today you let me see the manipulative David in relation to Alma. But then you fear that I will be manipulating *you* and taking advantage of you."

David now says that it's an illusion that he is going to fare better. He gives examples from his profession as to why things are so difficult. "Even the big companies are having problems," and so on. "That's the reality of my profession," he adds.

He continues to project the manipulative David into me and is trying to convince me that it is an illusion for me to expect that he will have anything for me in the future. He may also be using the *reality* of his profession to punish himself in order to assuage his unconscious guilt. I begin to interpret that he seems to be using reality to prove . . .

He interrupts. "Yes, it is possible. There *are* alternatives." He has mentioned viable alternatives to his profession and he does it again. He adds, "There is a part of me who doesn't want to move, though . . ."

I believe he doesn't want to move because of the unconscious fantasy outlined above, namely, a fear of being robbed if he does well.

David continues, "The other day a friend of mine called that he has a lot of work for me. But you have to present proposals and most of the time nothing comes of that. I told him, "Yes, I would think about it. But *no way* I'm going to waste my time with proposals that don't pan out." After a short silence he adds, "That's the aristocratic part of me, I know . . ."

He doesn't want to be in a situation where he might recognize his dependency on others and be subjected to rejection and psychic pain. In the transference this may mean that, acting out of his envy of me and out of his jealousy of my relationship with my husband or other patients, he doesn't want to give me anything: *"No way* I'm going to do something for you!"* He is back to his object usage and I become irritated, wishing to shake him out of his aristocratic stance: he is now the 'superior' one who needs from no one and is doing his own analysis. Remembering how he is using Alma, and probably fueled by my annoyance, I confront him with an important 'detail' he mentioned a couple of weeks ago: "You said you are making $500 a month and that means you *are* living off Alma." Annoyed, David argues, "No, it's about $1,500, which allows me to pay the rent and live.

I don't let him off the hook: "But you tell me $500 so that I get to pity you by thinking that you are in such a terrible shape. Then you can continue to use me." Seeming quite uncomfortable now, David adds softly, "Last year I made a total of $13,000."

Nearing the end of the session, David ponders, "I don't know what changed after my separation. Because I used to make good money before. Did *I* change or did *reality* change?"

He moves back in time as an evasion of the current situation, my interpretation and the guilt it is meant to stir up. If the reality changed, he is not accountable for what he is doing. I am left with the hopeless feeling that we lost whatever ground we had gained.

Tuesday Session

David starts off by telling me that yesterday he left the session *in bad shape* on two accounts: on the one hand because he realized that somehow he was using me. He would like now to find a way to pay me before his divorce becomes final. "I have to find a way," he adds. This afternoon, he wants to accelerate and finish some pending work so that he can get some money to pay me. After a silence, he says, "On the other hand I felt bad because having this kind of therapy is also my aristocratic thing. It's unrealistic in my situation to come four times a week."

Yesterday's session was not all wasted, I think. He is experiencing some guilt and the wish to make reparation. However, when he talks about his 'aristocratic thing' he is backing off. It may be unrealistic to have an analysis but I believe he is now saying this to deny the guilt, which undoes the reparation. If the situation is unrealistic, all he needs to do is stop—no need to look into what he is doing to me.

David continues: "Besides, I felt *very bad* realizing how I use women—that thing of living off Alma. Yesterday, I was calculating . . . it's not like that, I'm not living off Alma."

He is experiencing guilt again, followed by an immediate denial of guilt. Once again I could have zeroed in on how bad he felt when he realized how he uses women, and explore with him what that feeling bad felt like. In this way, I could have helped him bear the guilt by interpreting that the pain of the guilt due to his love of these women was evidenced in his immediate denial, not wanting to be a witness to what he did to them.

He now says: "Then, I was thinking that you don't give much importance to what I said before I left yesterday, about what changed after I left home. All my friends were tight financially and I always had money in reserve. The external situation changed, and I was asking myself yesterday to what extent this has to do with a feeling that my life has ended, that I don't have to support anyone, that I don't go out and fight. My life cycle ended with Vicky, and besides, my kids are no longer asking me for money."

He is now blaming the external situation for his actions and projecting his guilt into me: I ought to be feeling guilty for not giving it importance. The rest seem to be rationalizations to evade his guilt about living off Alma and me. Annoyed once again at his tactics, I interpret that clearly something changed after he left home. But he may be using the separation and the current recession in order not to feel guilty and as a way to expiate the guilt. I add, "The recession becomes your punishment for what you did to Vicky during the marriage and when you left her." I thus interpreted his expiating guilt through punishment. However, it would have been better had I brought him back again to his statement about how *bad* he felt using women and his difficulties in bearing this guilt. It was important that he understood that he felt so bad—guilty—because he also cares and wishes to make things better for us.

David replies, "Yes, I have noticed that. We Jews have a very guilty structure. Somehow, there is a part of me that says I committed a big crime and I have to pay for it." After a short silence he adds, "In spite of the fact that I feel much better I don't feel the push to look for other avenues." I now get irritated once again as I feel that we are back to square one. I interpret that the Jew's guilty structure means that his guilt is racial, not personal, and he is thus not accountable for what he does to Vicky, Alma, or me. He doesn't get away with this explanation, however. He alludes to guilt when he talks about having committed *a big crime*. That he has to pay for it, however, implies expiation of the guilt rather than reparation. Expiation bypasses the experience of guilt and makes reparation impossible. Maybe he is now expiating the guilt by paying for the crime as he listens to me and puts up with my 'scolding' him. He feels better with the help I have given him but cannot experience gratitude because he begrudges my capacity to help him. Since he cannot experience gratitude, he sees no need to look for other avenues to pay me. Fueled by my irritation, I focused on the defenses against guilt rather than zero in on his having committed a *big crime*. This might have enabled him to come into closer contact with his guilt feelings.

He continues, "I think that what happens is that I have not been able to differentiate between the neurotic guilt and the healthy part. You put the emphasis on the guilt, but you don't distinguish what type of guilt it is."

Even though he raises a valid point here, I sense that he is doing it to project the guilt for his using me onto me. It's all my fault—he is not getting the right help from me—and I should be the one to feel guilty. This may be both an envious attack on my competence and a projection of guilt where the guilt is being shifted onto the analyst.

In these first two sessions, David has used several defenses against an awareness of guilt, even though he has claimed, from the beginning of his analysis, that he was paralyzed by guilt. He *is* right, but only with regard to his enormous unconscious guilt and what happens when he interferes with its becoming conscious. David talks about his guilt but is not yet *suffering* his guilt, and therefore cannot properly repair his damaged internal objects and his external ones.

Early in the transcript one can see how David projects dependency and becomes a 'helper' to Alma's friend, a role he assumes in all his relationships. He took pride in helping his wife with her papers years ago and now is helping Alma with her professional writing; he also advises his male friends concerning their relationship problems. In the projection of dependency, he loses his infantile self in the other by becoming the mother. When free from this projection, he wakes up to realize he is not doing anything for himself.

In the story of the Monday session, the adolescent uses the older woman, gets into bed with her so that her fiancé finds them in bed. He escapes through a window, flaunting his psychopathic-like behavior that invites punishment from me. He seems to hold onto this view of himself as independent and uncaring because it helps him split off his infantile, dependent self. Later on, he says he tells women he needs his own life, he needs to generate an interest in his own house. This is again a way for him to get away from the baby part of his personality that may have no other interest than his mommy and who is desperate, or enraged in her absence. Early in the analysis, he dreamt about a cat and associated to a girlfriend's dog who had defecated all over the place when he had been left alone.

It is clear that when he talks about the guilt he feels toward Vicky, his ex-wife, or later, when he says he doesn't want to be a witness to all this, I failed to help David stay with this experience. Had he resisted it, that would have given me a chance to interpret his enormous anxiety about loving and being dependent on someone like Vicky or on me in the transference. I might have reminded him of the abandoned dog part of him and his fear of his infantile rage. One of the reasons why he manages to abandon his objects or make them wait unnecessarily is to put into them this needy, desperate, and enraged infant him.

When David displays and talks about his aristocratic syndrome, I take the bait and confront him with a detail, the $500 a month, which reveals that he is living off of Alma, his girlfriend. He seemed again to be flaunting his psychopathic-like attitude as a defense against dependency out of the fear of losing his present autonomy. I also suspect he *wanted* to be nailed in order to expiate his unconscious guilt about using his objects. It might have been better to point out to him his insistence on showing me how callous and uncaring he is about doing better for his objects. This might have led me to interpret his fear of becoming a dependent and enraged baby with no control over his objects and how he gets rid of this baby-part in the people close to him so that he can continue to play his aristocratic self that deludes him into believing that he does not need anyone.

As soon as David begins to experience some guilt over not wanting to look for other avenues to improve his income, he projects his guilt into me, suggesting I have not helped him distinguish the type of guilt he experiences. I imagine that in his mind he would like to believe that his guilt is neurotic, thus excessive and unrealistic, and that there is no need for gratitude or a wish to repair his objects.

To recapitulate, so far the transcript shows how the analyst's interpretations of the patient's evasions and other defenses against guilt can make the analyst fall prey to a sado-masochistic enactment in which the patient successfully projects his or her sadism and guilt into the analyst who may then *find* himself or herself scolding the patient. By doing this, the patient expiates the guilt and goes back to 'square one' with respect to an understanding of what he or she does to his or her objects. A patient's masochistic responses are easier to understand when they follow the incipient emergence of guilt and as a retreat from it and harder to detect when a patient like David uses the masochistic response prospectively to defend against the emergence of guilt.

Wednesday Session

David brought in two dreams with oedipal material. In one of them, *he is at a Kodak stand, asking them to develop some Polaroid film. Two women were rubbing their bodies against him while his friend, Charlie, was looking at him disapprovingly. He was afraid Charlie would tell Alma about this.* In the second dream, *he was with Peter, Alma's brother. Peter was recklessly driving David's car while David, sitting next to him, was trying to control him with no success. Peter forced an oncoming car to go off the side of the road.*

In his associations to the dreams, it became evident that Polaroid represented instant gratification, whereas Kodak stood for his capacity to wait. In the process of seeking instant gratification with the mother, who, in the two women, is depicted as the breasts wanting *him,* he destroys the father, who is represented by the oncoming driver. David associates that after making love with Alma, he had visited a deli, giving a beautiful woman there his name and telephone number while the deli's owner was looking on. He had experienced a sense of danger doing this. I interpret that Peter, driving the car in a reckless way, represents the greedy and dependent part of himself who is now, after taking possession of the mother, out of control. David claims to see in Peter aspects of himself he dislikes. The oncoming car represents his father who is forced off the side of the road. Charlie stands for this displaced father and in the dream, he looks at David with a sad expression on his face. Alma and David had recently invited Peter for dinner and, as Peter left, he also seemed to David to express infinite sadness. I interpreted that the sad Peter stands for the sad little David that underlies the manic oedipal machinations in the dreams. The sad Charlie represents his awareness of having damaged his father and conveys David's guilt.

David's response to these interpretations was to wonder why he should go after a woman *precisely* after having made love to Alma, which had been so lovely. This takes us back to the Polaroid dream and his search for manic solutions when he realizes he cannot control his objects. The manic solution ends up becoming an attack on the woman and on the parental couple, which puts the relationship with Alma in jeopardy. I interpret that he is now questioning why he would betray Alma when there is no reason to retaliate. This means that he has no reason for attacking Alma other than his own hatred of her for his inability to control her and make her loving toward him whenever he wants. This takes us back to the Polaroid dram and his search for manic solutions when he realizes he cannot control his objects. The manic solution ends up becoming an attack on the woman and on the parental couple, which puts the relationship with Alma in jeopardy. It is also clear that he is afraid of intimacy and the natural dependency on his objects.

As we can see, this session is full of David's manic defenses against his dependency on the mother, in Alma, in Vicky, in me. The dreams reveal his internal struggle between omnipotent and more mature solutions to dependency. His guilt about the attacks on his father is experienced in projected form in Charles and Peter. I believe that an oedipal dream in this session represents a development because of the love for the mother implicit in it. Along with his guilt for the sad Charlie standing for his damaged father, and the implicit love for the mother in the dream, there is an incipient experience of guilt toward the mother when he ponders why should he go after women precisely after having made love to Alma.

Friday Session

In this session, the last of the week, David is finally able to experience some guilt. He tells me he woke up at 2:30 AM with an earthquake and an anxiety attack that lasted for a while. Then he tells me he had had a difficult day yesterday and had been tempted to call me. He didn't know where to turn. The situation with his pending divorce had come to a head as he had had to hire a lawyer in response to Vicky having hired one. He had not told her of his action, which he sees as a retaliation and as knifing Vicky in the back. David had hung up the phone on Vicky even though she was no longer angry and sounded sad. He said he felt very guilty about this and associated again to the circumstances under which he left the marriage. David recounted this story with more details this time around, bemoaning the ugliness of the way he left, without any warning and through the back door. This led him to review the circumstances under which he left his country while his children were being held by the police, something he had not told me before. In acute pain he exclaimed, "I can't believe I *did* that!"

David described his feelings toward Vicky as they were raising their children and his being upset at her lenient ways with them, and at her wanting to take them along everywhere while he wanted to leave them at home. It became clear how displaced David felt by his children. He had never said anything to her about his jealousy but surrounded himself with friends so that they were seldom alone as a couple. She had not complained about this to him either. At some point he poignantly said,

"We never gave ourselves a chance!" David remembers Vicky saying she didn't understand why he was so resentful of her. He tells me of his early resentment that she was a professional with two jobs, owned a car, while he still needed a year and a half to graduate. He adds that he tried to "play up his dependent thing" by fantasizing being supported by her. But suddenly, his rage at her becomes clear when he exclaims, "I marry this gal and she gives me her tit but later this gal *doesn't* give me her tit!" More calmly, he later adds that that is probably where the resentment lies. I remind him of his jokes about the patient that follows him in the hour and how he feels displaced by her. David acknowledges that he jokes about that but now states that his resentment is real and compares his feelings with the patient before him and the one who follows him. This brings him back again to his resentment with Vicky and about the ugly way he abandoned her through the back door. His voice lowers and he utters slowly, "This is very sad. . . . This is very painful."

DISCUSSION

The Wednesday session is full of David's manic defenses against his dependency on the mother in Alma, in Vicky, in me. The dreams reveal his internal struggle between omnipotent and more mature solutions to dependency. His guilt about the attacks on his father is experienced in projected form in Charlie and Peter. I believe that an oedipal dream in this session represents a development because of the love for the mother implicit in it. Along with his guilt about the sad Charlie standing for his damaged father, and the implicit love for the mother in the dream, there is an incipient experience of guilt when he ponders why he should go after women precisely after having made love to Alma. Only on Friday, the last session of the week, does David consciously experience the guilt resulting from his attacks on his mother. Here, he is able to revise his account of abandoning Vicky and of his leaving his country and abandoning his children, adding further painful details to a story he had told me at the beginning of the treatment. This suggests that in spite of the various defenses against guilt he had resorted to earlier in the week, there appears to be a gradual increase in his capacity to tolerate it.

Some remarks about my countertransference are in order here. As I stated earlier, the analyst may fall prey to a sado-masochistic enactment because of the analyst's *own* guilt toward the patient as a frustrating object. In *Transference and Countertransference*, Racker (1968) points out how the oedipal situation of the analyst will express itself in every countertransference. And for him, "Although the neurotic reactions to countertransference may be sporadic, the predisposition to them is continuous" (p. 111). This argues that there is a basic depressive situation that the analyst needs to work through in each analysis. In addition to his oedipal frustration, David's pseudo-psychopathic attitude of not caring for his objects and his evasive responses with regard to his guilt toward these objects and toward me account for a possible unconscious hatred toward him that may have fueled my attempts at cornering and 'nailing' him with evidence of his using or abusing them.

My unconscious hatred of David as a rejecting father is further increased by my identification with the women in his life who must also represent in my unconscious my rejected and damaged mother. In his evading guilt and reparation, I am threatened with a catastrophe: my encounter with my destroyed mother. Thus, there is something else at stake for me in trying to help David experience his guilt and repair his objects. By being fair and loving to Vicky, Alma, or me in the transference, he is restoring *my* internal damaged objects. His unwillingness to do this may increase my unconscious hatred even more, all of which must increase my unconscious guilt toward him, which contributes to a masochistic surrender to his neglect, creating a sado-masochistic situation. This is probably related to my having allowed his debt to me to increase so that, in not getting paid, I can expiate my guilt toward him by being punished.

Returning to the technical considerations concerning guilt, one could say that rather than focusing on the defenses against the emergence of conscious guilt, the analyst may need to focus on the patient's incipient experience of guilt, whenever and however fleetingly it appears in the material. This certainly follows Klein's dictum of going for the point of maximum anxiety. The analyst may need to bring the patient's attention to that moment in the session where guilt was experienced, acknowledging how painful it must be to recognize neglect or damage toward loved ones or toward the self. Just as the analyst attempts to get the patient to describe his or her anxiety in *detail* (Gooch, 1992) in order to help the patient make contact with his or her experience, the analyst may need to ask for the *details* of the experience of guilt and, by his listening to him or her, help the patient to bear it. However, no matter how helpful this 'containing' of the patient's pain is as an initial step, it does not alter the unconscious dynamics. This step might elicit new associations which then may allow the analyst to interpret the underlying dynamics. The internal situation will only be altered by interpreting the ways in which the patient attempts to 'cure' himself or herself of guilt, which tend to perpetuate or increase it. Such interpretations of the patient's defenses against the experience of guilt provide an *anchor* that prevents or delays a shift back to the paranoid-schizoid position where guilt seems to turn into persecution.

The importance of bearing the guilt is that it will enable the patient to repair his or her internal objects and thus to make changes in his relationships to external ones. This will have the effect of reducing the patient's depression, which has to do with his or her having damaged internal objects. As Rey (1986, 1988) maintains, patients ultimately come to analysis to get help in repairing their damaged internal objects. This requires that the patient increase his or her capacity to stay in the depressive position. Klein's (1948) statement regarding the *simultaneous* appearance of anxiety, guilt, and reparation supports this notion of technically giving guilt, as one gives anxiety, a primary focus of an interpretation.

When attacks on the object due to envy or jealousy are acknowledged, unconscious guilt becomes conscious and this conscious guilt becomes more bearable. On the other hand, the patient's idealization of destructiveness and ruthlessness will increase unconscious guilt, which decreases its bearability. In general, one could say that anything that devalues love as sentimental or weak will increase unconscious guilt, whereas interpretations that succeed in mobilizing love will decrease unconscious guilt and increase its bearability. Guilt is thus so critical because it embodies all the issues of love and hate. It must be worked through over and over since a new constellation of defenses may appear after an earlier one is interpreted (Mason, 1995). Mobilizing the love might have prevented a sado-masochistic enactment in the transference.

What has become apparent in David's analysis is that he cannot move fully into a depressive concern for his objects because of his unconscious envy and jealousy which makes him spoil and devalue them. His envy and jealousy are not apparent in the material presented but have been the focus of many earlier sessions. The hatred toward his objects arises from what he experiences as a narcissistic injury, the recognition of their goodness and how much he needs them. At present, his envy and jealousy, rather than his defenses against them, are being expressed more directly in the transference. One can hope that by making his envy and jealousy conscious and by his *experiencing* them rather than merely talking *about* them, as he often does, he will be able to prevent them from becoming destructive. This will not only spare his external objects of his attacks on them but will diminish his attacks on his internal objects. The devalued, spoiled internal object perpetuates his fear that, as he puts it, "I don't have what it takes," thus maintaining the ruthless solution of exploiting his objects. Once his envious attacks and his attacks due to jealousy diminish in scope and intensity, he may be able to experience more fully the guilt for such attacks, a loving concern for his object, and a move toward reparation. The clinical challenge was to help David experience conscious guilt and perhaps most difficult, to confront the issue of reparation.

FIVE

Guilt: Some Theoretical and Technical Considerations

Robert Kravis, Psy.D.

In discussing Desy Safán-Gerard's contribution, I would like to start with some general comments about theory and how it informs the analyst's organization and understanding of the data. Then I will discuss the concept of guilt, and finally talk about the case material she has so generously offered us. It is my hope that these topics will overlap and provide a basis for further discussion of her excellent contribution.

I am a classical analyst. When I looked at the title of this paper I anticipated that discussing it would be challenging in that I expected that it would be akin to discussing a paper written in a foreign language. To my surprise I discovered that I understood and agreed with much more than I had expected to. Although there are some areas of significant difference which I shall point out as I go along, I have come to believe that there may be much more in common in classical and Kleinian theory and practice than is commonly realized.

WHAT IS THE GOAL OF AN ANALYSIS?

I will take as my starting point the goals of analysis. Dr. Safán-Gerard mentions that some Kleinian analysts, I think she would count herself among them, see the goal of analysis as being the "repair of damaged objects." At first blush this seemed to me to fall into the category of the foreign language I mentioned earlier. But it is important to consider that patients, like all of us, introject objects during the course of development. And further, that some of these introjects are distorted as a function of an

59

immature perceptual and cognitive apparatus, while others might be more accurately perceived flawed objects themselves, hence, a classical analyst might be viewing what Dr. Safán-Gerard is calling "damaged objects" as distorted or flawed introjects. Additionally, regarding the question of their 'repair,' classical analysts often observe that object representations change during the course of an analysis. We would say the introjects are modified. But would a classical analyst say that this is the goal of analysis? I think not. Rather, a classical analyst might say that the goal of analysis is to analyze unconscious conflicts and that if this is accomplished, self and object representations are modified as a by-product of this work. Additionally, I think there is a difference in the Kleinian view of how damaged objects get repaired. Although Dr. Safán-Gerard was not specific about this, it seems to me that she is suggesting that the original damage is caused by hate and that there is a split between love and hate that must be undone through their unification or perhaps reunification in order for the object to be repaired. She does specifically state that when love and hate are both experienced, guilt comes into conscious awareness, but more about that later.

Regarding the modification of introjects, a classical analyst might consider that both self and object representations are established in layers during the course of development and further that the regressive process of analysis allows for an examination of them as they emerge into conscious awareness. In the analytic situation they can then be reworked and modified as their genetic and dynamic meanings are interpreted, understood, and worked through. The developmental component of this formulation infers that in addition to perceptual and cognitive immaturity, self and objects are viewed and introjected through the lens of the developmental conflicts attendant to the psychosexual phases through which the individual progresses, and that all this takes place outside conscious awareness.

These considerations reveal a significant difference in how Kleinians and classical analysts think about both the goals of analysis and the technique of analysis. More about this in the discussion of the case. Perhaps it goes without saying that the theoretical perspective with which the analyst approaches the material will shape his or her understanding and interpretations of it. Specifically, one analyst is looking for evidence of damaged objects in the material while another is looking for the presence of unconscious conflicts.

DIFFERENT VIEWPOINTS

What about the understanding of guilt? As mentioned above, Dr. Safán-Gerard indicates that when love and hate are brought together, guilt comes in conscious awareness. She draws an important distinction between expiation and reparation. Expiation is essentially aimed at avoiding guilt, while reparation requires confronting it. Her discussion of defenses against guilt including projection, projective identification, and manic defenses shares common ground with a classical point of view as did her sensitivity to the transference-countertransference ebb and flow. But although there was some mention of the superego at the beginning of the paper, references to it were lacking in the discussion of the case material. This raises a question as to whether superego analysis plays a role in Kleinian analysis. It seems rather that the focus is on the vicissitudes of love and hate with guilt arising in circumstances in which the patient has hurt someone he or she loves. It is not clear to me whether such hurts refer to hurtful fantasies which are not actualized, or to actual damage done to an object, or perhaps to either of those possibilities. I think this makes an enormous difference; it is one thing to fantasize about getting rid of the same-sex parent in order to exclusively possess the opposite-sex parent, but it is another entirely to abandon one's children, and to betray and abandon one's wife. Dr. Safán-Gerard's patient makes a distinction between 'neurotic guilt' and other guilt, in the latter case probably referring to actual egregious behavior. He says at one point, referring to abandoning his children, "I can't believe I did that." It seems to me that 'neurotic guilt' should be treated very differently in analysis than actual misdeeds because the former is a fantasy constellation while the latter is reality based.

This brings up a consideration of what it is that actually does allow for a person, in this case Dr. Safán-Gerard's patient, to abandon his children and to betray and abandon his wife. A classical approach to this question might start with the possibility that something is awry in this patient's superego development. Specifically, in an intact superego organization such behaviors would not be permitted. Prohibitions would intercede before impulses could be acted upon. In this patient's case, there is some information to help with this question. Dr. Safán-Gerard reports that the patient felt 'displaced' by his children. One might infer that they were seen by the patient as having taken his wife away from him. This might well have engendered hostility in the patient directed at both his wife and his children. Perhaps his rage was such that normal superego prohibitions were ineffective, resulting in his hurtful behavior toward all of them. In this scenario, it was perhaps the patient who himself felt abandoned and who then retaliated with abandonments of his own. This formulation would suggest that sensitivity to abandonment might be sought out in the patient's history. In fact, there is some evidence of this in the case report in the form of the patient's report that he was 'ill-treated' by his father, and that his mother, a busy physician, was 'mostly unaware' of this abuse.

A further issue in this case seems to be the cycling between crime and punishment. In fact, at one point, the patient mentions "there is a part of me that says I committed a big crime and I have to pay for it." He then follows this by saying, "In spite of the fact that I feel much better, I don't feel the push to look for other avenues." Exploration of what 'big crime' he has in mind would be important. One possibility is that this is an oedipal issue and as such the 'big crime' might be his wish to be rid of his father and to have his mother all to himself. Further, this strikes me as an illustration of precisely how the patient punishes himself by restricting his quest for success.

Here, Dr. Safán-Gerard's discussion of sadism and masochism in this patient and in the analysis is very much to the point. Her clear and detailed discussion, including the projection of both sadism and masochism into the analyst with resulting enactments, is compelling. But she approaches this material through the lens of hate, love, and reparation while I would see it as the patient's attempts to regulate guilt for crimes, real and imagined, by punishing himself or by getting someone else to punish him. Examples of this include the marked deterioration in his income following his leaving his wife for another woman, and his putting his analysis in jeopardy by accumulating a debt while acknowledging that he is not trying as hard as he might to find ways of generating income. He puts his analyst in the difficult position of either interrupting his analysis (sadism, making him the victim), or continuing to treat him without pay (masochism). In this formulation, the patient is enacting an unconscious conflict in which he feels injured, retaliates, feels guilty, seeks punishment (to expiate the guilt), and then, when the scales are balanced, starts this process over again.

NUANCES OF THE CLINICAL MATERIAL

The question would then be why he does this, which brings us to the session material. Dr. Safán-Gerard reports that the early analysis was focused on her patient's promiscuity, "and we spent time analyzing his anxiety about depending on a single object." Is there evidence that this was the nature of his anxiety or is this an assumption based on theoretical orientation? I ask this question because it seems at least equally plausible that the patient was engaged in making conquests, perhaps as a means of supporting his masculine prowess as a defense against feeling like a little boy. Dr. Safán-Gerard reports that the patient sees "women at the center and men around them as boys." And there is mention in the paper of the patient "constantly showing off with his analytical sophistication as another 'conquest.'" Might he not be engaged in an attempt to make his analyst another of his conquests? Could not the analyst be seen as a powerful woman who might be seduced and stolen away from her husband? Dr. Safán-Gerard mentions "a primitive oedipal constellation where mommy and daddy are felt to be enjoying each other and abandoning him" and views the patient's response to this perception as "an attack on the parental couple" resulting in "destroyed internal parents." I am not sure what the word 'primitive' refers to in this formulation, but I, too, thought of an oedipal constellation from which the patient feels excluded. But is his wish to destroy the parents or to intrude into their relationship? Might the patient's 'attack' be seen as a wish to have what the parents have, that is, an exclusive relationship with one of them? If so, this would represent a garden variety oedipal constellation in which the wish is to be rid of the father and exclusively possess the mother. However, with this patient, given what history we have, it seems that the mother would not likely be seen by him as someone who might be receptive to his wishes. It is reported that there was a maid who was maternal toward the patient and of whom he was fond. This woman might have been seen by the patient as an oedipal substitute, but his presentation suggests that she was an inadequate one. For it seems that one aspect of the patient's dynamics is his constant pursuit of the oedipal mother; a pursuit that he makes sure is doomed to end in failure as a means of replicating the original situation. I would speculate that one reason he cheated on and ultimately abandoned his wife was that he could not tolerate being an oedipal victor. The unconscious scenario required that he fail in his quest for happiness in love so he had to ruin his marriage. The same dynamic is likely being played out in his analysis where he also cannot allow himself to be successful. Dr. Safán-Gerard mentions in several places that she was encouraged to see the emergence of oedipal material as it indicated a love for the mother. But what if the patient views this as a love doomed to failure? And what about his wish to kill off his father in order to attain the mother? Clearly the oedipal constellation contains both aggressive and libidinal wishes. Further, are there any indications that oedipal issues are manifested in the transference? Dr. Safán-Gerard conveys that the patient at times deadened the analysis through intellectualization and distancing mechanisms. Perhaps he was regulating the degree of intimacy with his analyst. But the more current material is mainly characterized by sado-masochism alternating in both patient and analyst. Might there be some erotic component in the sado-masochism? In fact, we hear nothing about the erotic transference which one would expect in patient with such a history of womanizing.

Thoughts about the transference lead to consideration of the countertransference. I appreciated Dr. Safán-Gerard's willingness to consider this topic in her paper. However, I felt this section of the paper to be less compelling than her careful parsing of her reactions during her report of the sessions with this patient. I found the discussion of her irritation at her patient and her observation of how this led her to be somewhat sadistically persistent with him more engaging. Perhaps this is because I do not really understand the concept of damaged objects. For example, when Dr. Safán-Gerard mentioned "destroyed internal parents" regarding her patient's oedipal constellation, what does this mean? Does the patient actually think of them as non-existent? In any case, I feel that the countertransference is more likely to be found in the exchange between analyst and patient in this case.

A DEVELOPMENTAL PERSPECTIVE

With the above discussion in mind, a developmental perspective on guilt might be considered. Classical analysts view guilt as a hallmark of super-ego development, and view the superego as the 'heir to the Oedipus complex' (Freud, 1923). While there is evidence of children internalizing parental prohibitions prior to the oedipal phase of development, it is widely held that violations of such prohibitions do not generate guilt, but rather fear of being caught and chastised by external authorities, usually the parents. Such early internalized prohibitions would be considered to be superego precursors. Some classical theorists suggest that it is the internalization of parental authority that marks the establishment of the superego, as authority shifts from an external to an internal locus. The patient in this paper is male, so the mechanism for the establishment of the superego in the boy will be considered here. As the boy moves from a dyadic relationship with the mother, to a triadic involvement with both parents, the oedipal complex develops. The boy shifts his relationship to the mother from pre-oedipal primary object to romantic love object. The father is seen as the boy's rival in pursuit of his wish for exclusive possession of the mother. However, there are several dangers in this pursuit. One of these is the fear of retaliation from the father, castration anxiety. This is the danger most commonly considered as the impetus for the boy's resolution of the Oedipus complex. Specifically, his worry about retaliation leads him to abandon his wish to possess the mother and to identify with the father in the hopes of someday acquiring a spouse like his father's. But Dr. Safán-Gerard calls attention to another danger for the oedipal boy: his ongoing love for the father stands in conflict with his wish to be rid of him. Here, her discussion of the split between love and hate is very much to the point. In at least some cases, it is likely that the primary motive for resolution of the Oedipus complex may be a wish to resolve that conflict in favor of love by abandoning the oedipal rivalry. In addition, it is important to consider that the boy comes to appreciate that his pursuit of the mother is unlikely to be successful not just because the father stands in the way, but also because the mother conveys that she is already spoken for. As the boy renounces both aggressive wishes toward the father and libidinal wishes toward the mother, prohibitions against such wishes are established in the newly formed superego. Transgressions in the form of violations of these prohibitions both in fantasy and in deeds generate guilt, which appears for the first time at this point in development. It is important to consider that the superego has both libidinal and aggressive qualities. While it generates guilt as a consequence of transgressions, it also generates good feeling when internal standards and ideals are met. Early on, the superego is rigid and primitive in efforts to regulate both drive expression and self-esteem. Parental authority tends to be characterized in absolutes which become more sophisticated and nuanced over time. Superego contents are formed through the introjection of parental and other external sources, but the function of the superego is to regulate drive expression and self-esteem, not just to assure that the child conforms to societal norms and expectations.

All this can be applied to the understanding of Dr. Safán-Gerard's patient. To do so, one would have to consider the patient's material from both a conflictual and a developmental perspective. As mentioned earlier in my discussion, abandonment themes may play a role in his dynamics. If so, the reported lack of engagement from his mother together with the reported abuse from his father may have colored the patient's pre-oedipal development in a manner that affected his oedipal constellation. An abusive father may have exacerbated castration anxiety and may have reduced the patient's libidinal attachment to his father. While the former may have propelled the patient toward oedipal resolution, the latter may have interfered with the usual identification with the father. Further, the unavailability of the patient's mother may have made the prospect of oedipal engagement with her remote. Therefore it is likely that the patient ended up with a skewed oedipal resolution and a distorted superego. Specifically, as was mentioned earlier in my discussion, the patient can be seen as re-enacting his doomed quest for the oedipal mother by making repeated conquests which must then fail. In other words, the libidinal prohibitions against incestuous wishes toward the mother are not fully in place. Rather, they are expressed and then quashed. In terms of superego activity, the initial expression is not curtailed, but the punishment for their expression is exacted. Considering the role of the father in this patient's oedipal constellation, it is stated in the paper the patient currently has no use for the father except insofar as the father provides him with money. Identification with the father seems to be lacking, except in the patient's repetition of the father's abuse as it is expressed both in his relationship with women and toward himself. In terms of superego activity, once again the original prohibitions against expression of aggressive impulses are lacking, but self-imposed punishment in the form of failure in both love and work is apparent.

In a skewed superego organization it is not surprising to find that role of guilt is complicated. Dr. Safán-Gerard points to fleeting moments of guilt in the session material from which the patient quickly retreats defensively. His ability to 'bear' the guilt or to 'bear witness' to his transgressions is limited. In fact, I believe that it is difficult to determine whether he is actually feeling guilty, or is feeling sorry for himself. In other words, is he feeling guilt or narcissistic depletion? He does express incredulity when considering his abandonment of his children, but when he considers the situation with his wife, he comments, "we never gave ourselves a chance." This statement does not acknowledge his affairs and ultimate abandonment of his wife and children as events for which he bears responsibility.

In my view, the analytic task with this patient is to clarify this question of guilt or narcissistic depletion. To do so would, from a classical point of view, require superego analysis. What I have in mind here is an inquiry in the analysis into pre-oedipal and oedipal aspects of the patient's early relationships with both parents. The starting point for this exploration would be the transference which, judging from the sessions reported, is rich with helpful material. Over the course of time in the analysis reconstructions could be made as a means of helping the patient come to understand how he came to be the person he is now. This must be done in a gradual manner to attempt to avoid intellectualizations and other distancing mechanisms at which this patient is quite adept. It may be noted that what I am suggesting does not refer to self and object representations directly. But my recommendations have to do with how this patient treats himself and his objects, which I believe is determined by his personality organization in general and by his superego in particular. For this patient, I believe that this approach is the key to a successful analysis.

CONCLUDING REMARKS

Approaching conclusion, I would like to say a bit about the title of Safán-Gerard's chapter. The idea that one feels guilty when one hurts a loved one makes sense to me. But can one also feel guilty for other reasons? What about hurting a stranger in an auto accident, committing 'victimless' crimes, viewing pornography, etc.? What about guilt for incestuous wishes or for sexual feelings or masturbation? In at least some of these examples there is no object available to whom to make reparation. Why wouldn't the recognition that one has hurt a loved one make one feel more guilty? And the question I raised earlier, what is to be done with egregious acts, as the ones in this case, about which the patient should feel guilty? Are we, as analysts, supposed to help repair that guilt also? It seems to me that in those cases the analyst's job is to help the patient understand the motives that led him or her to behave egregiously in order to facilitate change in the hope of interrupting the repetition of such behavior. And what might make the guilt bearable for the patient is the non-judgmental and caring demeanor of the analyst. This patient is lucky enough to have such an analyst. The patient, at one point, says that he does not want to 'bear witness' to his own guilt, but his analyst's ability to bear witness to it without condemnation allows and even encourages him to do so. But this is no small task. I imagine that it would be difficult for anyone listening to this patient's material to be non-judgmental and caring at all times, both because of the things the patient has done and because of his assault on the analyst and the analysis. Furthermore, I am not certain about this patient's capacity to love. He certainly cannot possibly love all the women with whom he has been promiscuous. And when he expresses distress about losing his marriage, is it because he loves or loved his ex-wife or because he feels sorry for himself after having ruined his chances for success in love? Is there evidence that he loves his analyst or is he using her like he has used other women, namely as a means of regulating his narcissistic economy?

I will end this discussion with several more general questions about Kleinian analysis, knowing full well that there is much we will not have time to get to: What is the role of the structural model in Kleinian analysis? Specifically, in addition to self and object representations, is there consideration of ego and superego development? Are reconstruction and genetic interpretations a part of Kleinian analysis? There was little discussion of the history of this patient. Is that because the discussion was purposely limited, or is history not such an important consideration in Kleinian analysis? Kleinian analysis has come to be considered as focusing on pre-oedipal development. Is that a fair representation? What is the role of the oedipal complex in Kleinian thinking? I want to thank Dr. Safán-Gerard once again for such a stimulating paper and am looking forward to further discussion.

SIX

Guilt in the Therapist and Its Impact Upon Treatment[1]

Stanley Coen, M.D.

The superego of the analyst at work, a relatively neglected topic, is addressed. The optimal superego stance for the analyst at work is to use himself, including his needs, wishes, and temptations, in order to understand himself in the service of helping his patients. To do so, the analyst needs to be overseen, guided, criticized, restrained, praised, and loved by his superego. Superego signals help to guide him. He needs to be convinced that he will not act on his temptations because of his ethical, loving stance toward himself and toward his patient and because, most of the time, he feels he can manage the passions in the consulting room. Colleagues are encouraged to scan themselves and to identify with analysts in trouble, in their descriptions, so as to rehearse catching potential vulnerabilities, needs, and desires at work with analysands.

The superego of the analyst at work has been insufficiently considered. Instances of boundary violations and ethical misconduct in our field leave no doubt that many of us run into problems which we don't anticipate when we enter the field of psychoanalysis. Colleagues' difficulties can scare and pain us, make us want to pull back, to close ourselves off emotionally. This is understandable but counterproductive. Gabbard (1995), Gabbard and Lester (1995), and Celenza (2007) believe that all of us can be at risk to cross or violate our patients' boundaries when we are sufficiently needy and vulnerable. Analysts are at much greater risk of crossing or violating their patient's boundaries in nonsexual ways (Coen 2007).[2] This chapter will not focus on analysts' boundary violations but on how the analyst's superego should best function at work.

The optimal superego stance for the analyst at work is to use himself, including his needs, wishes, and temptations, in order to understand himself in the service of helping his patients. The more tolerant the analyst can be of what he finds in himself, the more tolerant and helpful he can be with his patient. Intolerance in the analyst tends to lead to intolerance of the patient. For the analyst to be able to tolerate his needs, wishes, and temptations, he must be confident that he can contain them, not lose control of them, not enact them with his patient. Analysts gain such confidence by allowing themselves repeatedly to feel such longings deeply, when they are alone and when they are with their patients, learning thereby that these longings can be subsumed within their mature, responsible self. It is reassuring to keep discovering that feelings and wishes can be temporary and reversible, that we can go in and out of them without becoming trapped forever in one fixed position. Then temptations—regressive, incestuous, murderous—are only temptations rather than a prelude to ominous action.

Of course, we can never be fully certain that this time we won't be led astray by temptation. Indeed, such anxiety about the fate of our temptations is helpful in protecting ourselves from misusing our patients. Analysts can get into trouble with their patients when they are not made anxious by their temptations with their patients and do not say 'no' to themselves about enacting them. Jacobs (Panel, 2006) described a group of analysts who became sexually involved with patients; these analysts had been overindulged as children without their parents having set clear limits for them. Their training analyses did not deal with their absent limits and repetitive entitled wishes. Superego signals are helpful to the analyst at work to restrain, contain, and guide him. Superego signals refer to feelings and attitudes that help the analyst to manage his needs, wishes, and temptations toward his patients. Examples of the analyst's superego signals include: anxiety, guilt, self-criticism, shame, attitudes of restraint and limitation about his own childlike longings, with reminders of concern that his patient's needs, not his own, must be primary. Superego signals can be thought of as potentially helpful advice from the moral advising, restraining, punishing, loving, guiding part of ourselves. Helpful superego signals do not cause the analyst to become obsessively tormented about misdemeanors and transgressions—unless he is at such risk.

The analyst's superego at work needs to help and support him in his struggles in the consulting room for the sake of his patient's treatment. It needs to help him examine his own feelings, needs, and desires, and those of his patient, for the latter's sake. It needs to guide, restrain, tolerate, praise, and criticize what the analyst is able to observe about himself and his patient. A tolerant, loving attitude toward the analyst's affective experience enables him to help his patient to tolerate, and then to modify and resolve, conflict. This tolerant attitude can apply to what the analyst fears and hates in himself, but needs to bear, in himself and in his patient, for the sake of this patient's treatment. There certainly are limits to what analysts can bear to feel in themselves while at work with their patients, as we can easily see in supervising candidates. Candidates who have only just begun to analyze their childlike neediness, vulnerability, and hatred may find it intolerable to bear their patients'. This has been especially striking in the supervision of two pregnant candidate analysts whose patients were intensely stirred up by the analyst's pregnancy and her maternity leave (see also Imber, 1995). These two pregnant candidate analysts felt better able to stand their patient's needy, hateful wishes to invade and destroy the analyst's pregnant body, at least for a while, after attending the discussion group on 'The Pregnant Analyst' at the American Psychoanalytic Association. Each candidate analyst felt supported by other women analysts who had worked with patients while pregnant. Each candidate was able to keep such a supportive presence within her temporarily that encouraged her to tolerate her patient's clamor.

Many analysts, not just candidates, may require such ongoing affirmation in order to be able to stretch themselves so as to tolerate the heat in the consulting room. This contribution aims to highlight and support the helpful, guiding aspect of the analyst's superego that needs to tolerate what is most difficult for the analyst to bear. Some public presentations give the impression that analytic work can go effortlessly. This myth adds greater pressure to the analyst to push away his own disturbances at work rather than to draw upon them. More public presentation of analysts' struggles in the consulting room could help colleagues prepare for and tolerate their own difficulties. Then analysts are more likely to seek consultation for such disturbance, potentially reducing the risk of analysts misusing patients. Gabbard agrees with this strategy (personal communication, January 2011).[3]

One way of preparing ourselves for potential trouble in the consulting room is to identify with 'the analyst in trouble,' imagining ourselves in the shoes of colleagues who are in difficulty with patients, which they describe. Analysts are in trouble when they become stuck over an extended time in a patient's treatment, unable to extricate themselves from what is wrong so as to address it with their patient. Of course, enactments must happen in any treatment. Ordinarily, analysts are able to recover their analytic perspective relatively rapidly after an enactment. The analyst is in trouble when he cannot do so, when he cannot see what he has become caught up in and perpetuates it. Vignettes of analysts in trouble may reveal what is in the analyst's way with this particular patient—or at least the reader or listener can imagine his way into the clinical scene so as to grasp his own potential vulnerability and disturbance. This is a kind of practice analysis—practice at what is potentially difficult for a given analyst—so as to accept such difficulty with a bit

more readiness and equanimity. Readers or listeners can use colleagues'
clinical vignettes to imagine their own difficulties with such a patient.

You may not be so eager to follow this suggestion, as I have learned
from some colleagues to whom I have proposed it. Many of us automatically dissociate ourselves from analysts in trouble; we insist that we are
sharply different from them. It is preferable to believe, as many do, that
we have been well enough analyzed and trained that, as graduate analysts, we can be safely turned loose in the consulting room. It is so much
more threatening to keep focusing on our needs, vulnerabilities, and
temptations that can lead us astray. Yet that seems to be the best way to
help us catch our difficulties at work so that we can best help our patients. McLaughlin's (2005) openness is refreshing as he describes his
struggles to notice and manage interferences in his work with patients.
He vividly describes his efforts to explore his hesitation to resonate with
his patient's powerful homoerotic longings, the need to push away his
cravings for a man to love him. This had to be an impossible task given
that McLaughlin had been an infant when his father died. In order to
help his patient, he had more work of his own to do, work which helped
both analyst and patient. McLaughlin candidly acknowledged that he did
not analyze this in his two analyses. We need to consider how far we
have to go with such open, tolerant exploration of our child-like selves.

THE ANALYST'S LISTENING

Freud (1912) advised that the analyst "should withhold all conscious
influences from his capacity to attend and give himself over completely
to his 'unconscious memory.'. . . He should *simply listen*, and not bother
about whether he is keeping anything in mind" (emphasis added, p. 112).
"He [the psychoanalyst] must turn his own unconscious like a receptive
organ towards the transmitting unconscious of the patient. He must ad-
just himself to the patient as a telephone receiver is adjusted to the transmitting microphone" (pp. 115-116). Poet Robert Pinsky (2006)[4] advises
approaching a poem the first number of times one reads it by listening
only to the sounds, allowing oneself to reverberate with them, long before one tries to find meaning in the poem. Edward W. Tayler (2011),
Shakespearean scholar, invites us to 'behold and see'[5] and to listen to him
read Shakespeare's 'matchless poetry' in *Antony and Cleopatra* as we let
ourselves be carried away by its 'giddy oscillations.' This is what we
psychoanalysts hope to be able to achieve in listening to our analysands:
to allow ourselves to be carried away unconstrained by reason. Parsons
(2007) similarly uses Seamus Heaney's description of Heaney's (2002)
struggle to grasp T. S. Eliot's (1922) *The Waste Land* in order to recom-
mend Heaney's and his own preference for listening to sound in poetry
and with analysands. The goal is for the analyst to remain engaged with

the patient's and his own unconscious, rather than remove himself to more abstract levels of meaning. Chodorow (2003) differentiated 'listening for' from 'listening to.'[6] In the former, analysts search for what is familiar to them. In the latter, analysts try to grasp their patients' emotional worlds. Chodorow derives the term 'listening to' from Haydée Faimberg (1996) who listens to how her patients listen to her ('listening to listening'). Analysts in either mode of listening can connect with their patients' and their own unconscious, if they can allow themselves to do so. I believe that the less constrained the analyst is to find meaning in the analytic situation, the more able he will be to do so. Freud's view that the analyst should 'simply listen' could, but does not have to be, impeded by any kind of focused listening, whether it is 'listening for' or 'listening to.' For example, I tried to help a candidate supervisee listen to the noise in the consulting room that her patient generated. The patient would get herself and her analyst agitated as she complained loudly about what was wrong in her life. As my supervisee read process notes, I would encourage her to listen to the sounds rather than to search frantically for interpretations with which to placate her patient. My supervisee did not yet know her own vulnerability to being drawn in by her patient's desperate attempts to grab her attention.

Freud viewed the analyst as able to reconstruct the patient's unconscious from its derivatives which determine the latter's free associations. But then Freud (1912) warned that the analyst "may not tolerate any resistances in himself which hold back from his consciousness what has been perceived by his unconscious" (p. 116). What the analyst cannot see in himself, he cannot see in his patient. Freud is contradictory as he refers to 'psychoanalytic purification' (p. 116) but concedes that the goal is for analysts to 'become aware of,' not necessarily to resolve, their complexes which interfere with grasping their patients' communications. Freud (1913a) describes giving "myself over to the *current* of my unconscious thoughts" (p. 134, emphasis added) while listening to his patients. But he (1915 [1914]) is also worried that he and his followers may become too carried away by such currents of the unconscious: "The experiment of letting oneself go a little way in tender feelings is not altogether without danger. Our control over ourselves is not so complete that we may not suddenly one day go further than we had intended" (p. 164). Hence neutrality and abstinence are required.

LETTING GO

Freud's (1912) advice that the analyst reject conscious control in order to give himself over to his 'unconscious memory,' allowing his unconscious to resonate with his patient's 'transmitting unconscious,' emphasizes the analyst's need for access to his own unconscious life. Not only the patient but the analyst, too, has an unconscious with which he needs to resonate. Can we now let ourselves go sufficiently with our patients that we can resonate with their unconscious and with our own without risk of getting so carried away that we use our patients *primarily* for our own needs? We are painfully aware that some colleagues do not restrain themselves with their patients and misuse them. We would like to believe that we can resonate as fully with our patients' unconscious needs as we have to, that that is the job we must do. That is not always correct, even for the most capable analysts. We all have our needs and the vulnerabilities they engender. Parsons (2006) also notes analysts' ambivalence "to lay[ing] ourselves unconditionally open to ourselves" (p. 1186) in order to analyze our patients.

This is the reason to scan ourselves and to practice identifying with analysts in trouble—so that we can more readily grasp our own interferences as we view their difficulties. We have not established guidelines as to how far we can safely let ourselves go in our feelings, wishes, fantasies, and temptations with our patients. How sexually aroused can an analyst feel in an erotic transference with an attractive patient before becoming worried about sexual boundary crossing? How much murderous hatred should we feel with an angry, rejecting, negativistic patient, how much detachment, distance, unconcern with a distant, schizoid patient? How much should we want to share in a narcissistically impressive patient's specialness, talent, and celebrity?

Because we worry about crossing and violating boundaries in action with our analysands, we want to set limits to our wishes, feelings, and temptations. Denial and minimization of concern about transgression block us from appropriate anxiety in the face of imminent danger of boundary crossing and violation. Some degree of anxiety and mistrust of ourselves seems essential for protecting the analytic situation. So, we need to be wary of defensively using contentions like Jacobs's (2006), even if true, that the superego functioning and character of most analysts will not permit them to sexually violate their patient's boundaries. If indeed (see e.g., Wilson, 2003; Hirsch, 2007) our narcissistic needs influence what we want from our analysands, we will need to struggle against misusing them. If even our use of psychoanalytic theory can be in the service of our needs of our patients, we will need to refocus the treatment on our patients rather than on ourselves. And if much of our character is not even subject to our own conscious awareness, if it remains outside of our subjectivity (Kite, 2008), there has to be much that we cannot possibly manage.

THE ANALYST'S SCANNING (OF HIS OWN UNCONSCIOUS)

To grasp derivatives of unconscious processes in the affective force-field between them, to resonate with the patient's unconscious and his own, the analyst needs to scan himself just as he scans his patient and their interaction. To try to follow these bits of his own unconscious, the analyst can scan whatever he can catch within himself that lies outside of his easily available conscious awareness. He can scan his feelings, sensations, thoughts, concerns, images, fantasies, language, songs, daydreams, night dreams—whatever might be revealing with this patient. Each analyst resonates in his unique way. Analysts may respond with song or music in their head, with graphic or artistic images, with language, poetry, or texts, with body sensations or images of movement. Analysts can scan what they say and do with their patients for meanings beyond what is immediately available in consciousness.[7]

We know that colleagues differ widely in how much they scrutinize themselves at work. Some do so fairly consistently while others do so rarely, only when something seems to be significantly amiss. A generation of analysts were encouraged by Searles (1963) to do a 'no-holds-barred' search of their raw emotional reactions so they could survive treating their psychotic patients. Some adapted this technique to analyzing nonpsychotic patients although it is much less commonly described. We do not know whether those who scrutinize themselves consistently allow themselves more or less wish, fantasy, temptation with their patients than do those who scan themselves much less frequently. Analysts' self-observation may aid analyzing or take them away from being fully focused on their patients. The analyst's temptation may take him away from his 'free floating attention' to his patient's process (Parsons, 2000) or bring him closer to it, if this analysis requires patient and analyst to become caught up in temptation.

It is not clear how analysts are to tolerate what they can't stand in themselves so as to help their patients. What analysts cannot bear to see and preserve within themselves, they will be unable to keep finding in their patients (Stern, 2010). Then, Stern believes, enactments will occur with patients, that both express and hide what analysts cannot face. He uses Sullivan's (1953) concept of 'not me' to contrast the more forceful pressure in having to extirpate an aspect of oneself from merely pushing it out of consciousness (repression). With milder dissociation, not with stronger dissociation, Stern believes, another part of ourselves will be able to reclaim the horrifying, unbearable aspect of ourselves which we must so fiercely put outside of us. Caper (1997) advises us to hold onto our love of psychoanalysis and for ourselves as psychoanalysts in order to persevere with what is unbearable for analysts while analyzing. Bergmann (1997) believes that Freud's love for psychoanalysis 'immunized' him against sexual transgression. Our ethical stance, love of psychoanalysis, and multiple perspectives toward ourselves can and should help us tolerate what feels so repugnant within ourselves. But we have to be prepared for how difficult this must be.

Steiner (2000) noted, only in passing, that the term 'love for psychoanalysis' (Caper 1997, 1998) omits hatred for psychoanalysis. Similarly, Kanwal (2010) counterposed Levine's (2010) loving psychoanalysis with hating, disappointing, depressing, painful psychoanalysis. This has been a dangerous omission—in the use of the term and in our literature—to talk of loving psychoanalysis without also considering hating psychoanalysis. Love for psychoanalysis and for ourselves as psychoanalysts as well as for our patients can be overridden by hatred so that patients and our field can be harmed. It would help for us to discuss and bear our hatred for psychoanalysis as well as for our patients. From this chapter's perspective, we can hate psychoanalysis for the demands it places on us just as we can esteem it for asking us to know ourselves. Such self-knowledge is painful; we can resent the interminable challenge (Freud, 1937) to remain responsible for what we would rather eliminate from ourselves. We can hate psychoanalysis for asking us not to live out our dark side, but to acknowledge, contain, and manage it. That is the challenge in analysts' allowing ourselves to resonate fully with our patients' unconscious and our own, that to do so requires that we continually confront what we do not want to fully face in ourselves.

Analysts can be reluctant to reveal much about their own inner temptations and conflicts at work as if these could always be minimal, mild, and easily manageable. Even when there has been considerable effort to focus on the analyst's temptations, colleagues may minimize their discomfort (Panel, 2010), making it difficult for the rest of us to learn about what really goes on in the consulting room. A thoughtful colleague recalls another distinguished colleague's claim that you never hear the truth about an analyst's clinical work from the dais but only, as it were, in the back of the room.[8] Of course, analysts have reason to worry about the ill effects of disclosing their temptations, anxieties, and struggles at work with patients to colleagues. Some colleagues have forsworn ever presenting their clinical work again in public after having been attacked by others. Presenters can never know in advance how their self-revelations about their work will be received. Listeners and readers, even if correct, can be harsh.

From the perspective of the analyst's scanning himself, his temptations toward his patient may reveal much of what is at play between them. But first the analyst needs to filter out what is uniquely his own and unrelated to this particular patient. Otherwise, it is much too easy to attribute the analyst's temptations wholly to the patient, a kind of projective identification. For example, I found myself picturing Leo Stone before a second consultation with a colleague's analysand. Then, initially, while I was with the analysand, I continued to think about Leo Stone. I remembered my two consultations with him many years ago. I felt pleased with my growth as a psychoanalyst and wondered whether I was feeling competitive with him and with my colleague. But Stone's presence in my mind then reminded me of Stone's physicianly attitudes of warm caring, respect, and empathy. Now I could grasp that this was a message for my colleague, that her patient's harshly critical negativism had eroded my colleague's warm availability. Stone and my colleague came from the same psychoanalytic group, which Stone had influenced so positively. Sharing my musings with my colleague served to convey my advice to her.

Or an excellent supervisee did not show up for her supervision, nor did she call. The following day, I learned that her young children's caretaker had been unavailable; she had left a message. It was understandable that she would be overwhelmed with her child-care responsibilities. I like and admire this supervisee. I did not want to make my feeling dismiss her problem. In the next supervision session, she raised the possibility that she might have left the message at someone else's voicemail. With some hesitation, I said that would seem out of character for her. She spoke about pleasure and anxiety in completing her psychoanalytic training, anxiety about the eventual termination of her analysis. Another supervisor had told her she had pulled back emotionally with a patient, who was disconnecting from her, and with that supervisor. It became clear as she read her process notes that her patient had largely disengaged from her and from the analysis. Despite her suggestion, I didn't immediately grasp that this was a kind of parallel process (Gediman and Wolkenfeld, 1980), that I needed to feel blown-off by my supervisee so I could help her register, more fully, how blown-off by her patient she had been feeling. Now free to tolerate and use, with the help of supervision, how very angry she was feeling at her patient, she regained her position as a highly effective analyst with her very difficult patient.

Mr. R was highly negativistic and rejecting, more invested in what was wrong, in death and dying, than in opening up possibilities of caring and concern with others. Nevertheless, he seemed to allow himself to thaw, to come closer to me, and at times to his partner. He could not, would not, invest himself fully at work, resenting his critical, insufficiently nurturing (he felt) bosses so that he was told that he would lose his job. He again became much more negativistic, depressed, hopeless, critical that I and his treatment had not helped him sufficiently. His psychopharmacologist and I began to worry about him. He often missed his sessions, sometimes not even calling to say that he was not coming. I would become anxious and angry at feeling helpless and unsure about his safety. Contending that he felt worse about missing sessions, he reduced their frequency. But I also felt that I had to tolerate his needing to have more control over what was going on in his treatment. His struggle for power and control with me over the treatment intensified. When I interpreted his angry struggle with me over time and money (he would come ten minutes late to sessions and pay late), he angrily stated that he had made very clear to me that I was not to keep interpreting transference, and that I was not listening to him but rather doing what I wanted to do with him. My attempts to talk with him about how angry he felt that I, like his parents when he had been a child, had power over being and not being with him, led to arguments in which he tried to shut me up. I should just be supportive, his friend, and stop taking over from him. I could feel enraged, want to get rid of him, or wish that he see a different therapist, or kill himself, as well as feel worried about him. My initial efforts to talk about his trying to draw me in negatively by causing trouble, as he had done with his parents and bosses, led to intellectualized responses that he already knew this. It seemed to make a difference when I was able to feel more comfortable with his efforts to enrage me to the point where I would really want to come after him, not just destructively but also as a way of showing that I cared about him. He'd wondered earlier why he didn't feel good having me worry about his safety. He now began to talk once more about wanting a dominatrix to penetrate him anally, how good this felt physically. At first, this seemed, together with certain other activities he was engaging in, a counterpoint to what was wrong in his work with me. But there were clues in his telling about what he was not getting from his bosses, father, mother, partner, and me. Now I could imagine that I was to feel angry, pursue him, insist with him rather than back away, and then to fuck him anally. I was to be the father who shows, loudly and clearly, that he loves him and wants him. Once I could imagine this, I began to interpret it to him. He was now coming on time to the sessions, seeming less hopeless and negative, even about the end of his job. Now he was imagining possibilities. The sessions had a crispness, aliveness; we were 'on' with each other. When he spoke in an intellectualized way and I interpreted his hesitation to feel, he talked about growing up with both parents having been uncomfortable with feelings. He was opening up again emotionally with me. I responded to his talking about his mother's stiffness, his father's remoteness, and his own not feeling [his terms], by saying in a warm, inviting way, "Welcome to the playground of feelings!" He laughed appreciatively. We had reconnected. When he then began trying to decide whether he would go to a dominatrix later that day, I said, "Your wishes to be penetrated are now in this room." He spoke about the difficulty of involving his father emotionally. Then I could say how much he wanted me to come alive with him, to come after him emotionally, and fuck him. As the session was nearing the end, he became quiet. I asked what he was thinking; he answered eagerly that he wanted more. What a change this was from how he had been with me for so long!

In order to get there, I had to tolerate my murderous hatred for my patient, my wanting to get rid of him permanently, as well as to tolerate and preserve (in the face of my hatred) my love and desire with him. I had to be able to imagine ridding myself of him as well as feeling how much I wanted to again share an authentic, intimate relatedness with him. I had to imagine myself as the dominatrix who really does seem to care enough about him to *want* to penetrate him. And I needed to tolerate the homosexual longings for his father's love that made him uncomfortable. This is what I had to go through in order to be able to reach my patient. Of course, the emotional path would have been different for other analysts. It could have been tempting for the analyst to accept literally this schizoid patient's demand for space in the treatment, without *also* trying to bring these passions into the consulting room.

THE ANALYST'S SUPEREGO STANCE

A colleague chided me for the 'superego-ish' tone to my paper on narcissistic temptations (Coen, 2007), so different, she pointed out, from my more usual accepting attitude toward affects and needs. I responded that I intended to make the audience anxious about the potential for transgression when analysts become too excited by their patients, so that they can be better prepared to catch themselves. Some colleagues object that we need room, some of the time, to cross boundaries consciously and deliberately with certain patients without tormenting ourselves excessively about such therapeutic interventions (e.g., Friedman, 2007). These colleagues contend that too much superego-ish concern about transgression stifles analysts' freedom and creativity. That is certainly true. But too little superego-ish concern risks transgression. When we do such seemingly therapeutic boundary crossing, I would prefer to observe myself and my patient, for motivations that may lie outside of our immediately available conscious recognition. It needn't be either/or, helpful versus hurtful. But a change from the ordinary can stir up the unexpected.[9]

If the analyst has developed a relatively adaptive, flexible interaction with his superego, he can utilize superego signals constructively without becoming paralyzed or constricted. The analyst's relative confidence in his affect tolerance has to allow for slippage so that he is prepared to register superego signals that he is feeling threatened. Dogmatic conviction of analytic invulnerability would make an analyst useless, unable to resonate with his patients' vulnerabilities. Even when the analyst cannot enjoy the affects in the consulting room, when they threaten him, he still needs to be able to preserve his focus on what his patient needs from him. Analysts are at risk of harming their patients when they are unable or unwilling to attend to the ongoing analytic process. So I think that the more aware we can be of our own temptations to join our patients in patterns of relatedness that block their autonomy and progress, the more rapidly can we catch our wishes to go astray with them. I am still troubled that when I presented (Coen, 2000) "The Wish to Regress in Patient and Analyst," a discussant insisted that he never had such temptations and only one colleague confided to me that he had had such wishes. Is it significant that the colleague who denied wishes to regress subsequently got himself into ethical trouble?

Analysts can disregard what their ego and superego help them to observe about themselves. Many different rationalizations can be used. Hirsch's (2008) book, *Coasting in the Countertransference*, shows the analyst's catching himself avoiding painful feelings with patients. He presents such examples openly and uncritically, inviting his reader to imagine his own similar lapses without excessive shame and guilt. I like Irwin Hirsch's book. But from the perspective of the analyst's superego at work, I would want to encourage analysts to go further with their self-inquiry, to really grapple with their hindrances, or, if that is insufficient, to seek consultation. With Jill who had been "egregiously" abused sadistically by her father as a child, the analyst often felt sleepy, unable to connect emotionally with his patient. He could imagine that he was identified with her dissociation or with her mother's ignoring her abuse. This did not help him gain an empathic perspective on their interaction. He felt little sexual interest in her, relieved that he did not feel sexually exploitative with her. We cannot know what kept the analyst from having sexual or sadistic feelings with Jill. I want to use this vignette imaginatively, as this paper encourages, to try to feel my way into her father's role with her. I encourage you to join me in feeling your way into this difficult scene. I imagine feeling sexually sadistic with Jill so as to bring her trauma into the consulting room. This would be difficult but tempting for me to feel. If I felt disengaged from Jill, I might imagine that I was enacting a compromise between feeling and avoiding sadistic exploitation. I want colleagues to feel sufficiently troubled that they could not remain emotionally engaged with a patient who had been severely traumatized sexually to seek consultation.

I love Joyce Slochower's (2006) chapter "The Analyst's Secret Delinquencies." Slochower is an outstanding example of an analyst who attends responsibly to her own feelings. She criticizes herself for gazing at a photograph of her adorably smiling ten-year-old daughter during a patient's session; she contrasts the deliberateness of her gazing with reverie. She imagines her patient had not held her attention as he had not held his parents' attention. Could this be an example where the superego interferes too much? I want to use this lovely example fancifully to imagine that outside of such guilty self-criticism, the analyst could feel she wanted to help her patient feel what he, and now she, had missed of the joys of feeling like an adored and adorable child. Sure, the analyst was providing herself with something she was not getting from her patient. But this could be just the kind of example where we might relate the analyst's longing to what was going on right then between them. This could indeed have been sad and touching for both of them to have felt, had the analyst felt comfortable using her own affective experience with her patient. Nor would this necessarily have required self-disclosure, although I could easily imagine that with certain remote, closed-off patients, I might have wanted to get their attention and make contact by talking a bit about what had just happened with me. Here, Slochower reports her withdrawal from her patient. In other examples, she emphasizes analysts' use and misuse of patients. Such focus allows us to try to grasp what we now want from our patient.

HOW TO IDENTIFY WITH AN ANALYST IN TROUBLE: THE MASUD KHAN IN ALL OF US

Allowing ourselves to identify with an analyst in trouble can help us catch our potential vulnerabilities and difficulties. Here I want to draw just a bit on what I have written about using Masud Khan's writings (Coen, 2010c). We could see Khan as struggling to understand and manage his own difficulties *within his writings*, from which we could learn. By imagining their own difficulties within their patients, authors can imagine how to help their patients and imagine themselves being helped. The contradictions are jarring when it becomes clear that Khan could not contain himself so as to follow his own recommendations on managing his patients and himself.[10] Khan pressures his patient to reveal details about his trauma just after cautioning analysts to respect traumatized patients' need for control and protection. Khan could be very impatient. So can I. It was refreshing to hear Harold Blum say publicly that he could not have waited as patiently as Ed Weinshel to interpret his patient's budding transferences. I can want to practice feeling my impatience to engage a remote patient so as to lessen my uncertainty about the treatment, contrary to what my patient needs.[11] Then I am somewhat like Khan. Reading Khan's clinical work can help us to identify with an analyst's wanting to do his best, yet often unable to transcend his own needs and limitations. That applies not just to Masud Khan but to all of us. The better prepared we are to accept our needs and limitations, the better we function as analysts.

A patient who has missed a number of recent sessions returns sputtering that he can't stand to come to this treatment nor can he stand what is now so glaring in himself. He hates the needy, selfish, imperious child in himself who always wants: attention, coming first, not having to share. Thinking of Masud Khan, as well as about all of us including myself, I suggest—certainly not for the first time—that it would be more helpful for him to be able to manage this impossible kid within *himself, a task his father has been unable to accomplish. I tell him that this is a task we all need to tackle at some time in our life, especially when we haven't been helped to do so as children.*

Perhaps it is helpful for all analysts to acknowledge the Masud Khan within us rather than to so gleefully expel him from our ranks. But then we have to manage him responsibly, as best we can, subordinating his needs to our patients'. Then Masud Khan, and other analysts in trouble — which, some of the time, may be any of us — can be of help to all analysts. A loving, guiding, affirming, restraining, appropriately critical superego stance of the analyst at work should be able to manage the Masud Khan in us — some or much, but not all, of the time.

NOTES

1. Earlier versions of this paper were presented at the Michigan Psychoanalytic Society's Annual Conference, Novi, MI, 2010; Cincinnati Psychoanalytic Society, 2011; Florida Psychoanalytic Society, 2011; American Psychoanalytic Society, 2012.

2. Boundary violations in contrast to boundary crossings, according to the *Ethics Casebook of the American Psychoanalytic Association* (ed. Dewald and Clark, 2001), are repetitive, advance further, and are not dealt with analytically (see Coen 2007).

3. Harris (2009), and Harris and Sinsheimer (2008) encourage us to talk openly about our vulnerability with patients so as to normalize our anxiety and distress at work. The analyst's need and desire are influenced by shifts in power, mutuality, and asymmetry between the analytic couple (Celenza, 2010).

4. Pinsky draws on Paul Valéry's essay "On Speaking Verse" and suggests that Robert Frost says something similar in "The Figure A Poem Makes" (personal communication, February 2011).

5. Line 13, *Antony and Cleopatra*, Act 1, Scene 1, spoken by Philo.

6. Here Chodorow (2003) does an impressive job of trying out various ways of listening to patients, sometimes listening for what is there to be found, but she does not explicitly advocate "just listening" which is Parson's phrase (2007, p. 144). We could question whether it is possible for an analyst to "just listen" without internal directives that may not always be fully available in consciousness. Then, no matter how much we try to listen openly to our patients, our listening may still be guided by our preferences, no matter how much we try consciously to set them aside.

7. Ogden's descriptions of his use of reverie are excellent examples (e.g., 1997a and b). So, too, are Akhtar's (2011a) considerations of how to use Urdu poetry and words that come to his mind with patients. The Barangers' (2009) work, which I read after I completed this essay, encourages analysts to take a 'second-look' at the 'dynamic bipersonal field' between patient and analyst, as they would supervise a colleague. The analyst tries to catch elements of the *patient's* unconscious as they emerge within the field.

8. D. Silverman, personal communication, December 2009.

9. Clinical example in full version of this paper.

10. For example, see Khan, M. M. R. (1981). "La main mauvaise." *Nouvelle Revue de Psychoanalyse* 24: 5-51. English translation, "The evil hand,' in: *Hidden Selves: Between Theory and Practice in Psychoanalysis*. (1983). London, UK: Hogarth Press, 1989.

11. I report that in the full version of this paper.

SEVEN

Reflections on the Absence of Morality in Psychoanalytic Theory and Practice

Elio Frattaroli, M.D.

When Salman Akhtar first asked me to be a discussant at the 2012 Margaret Mahler Symposium, I naturally felt honored. When he told me that the general topic would be guilt, however, I felt suddenly uneasy. I wasn't sure I had anything useful to say about guilt. Although I had been writing and teaching for many years about the importance of painful emotions, I realized that I had never thought much about the particular emotion of guilt, at least not in any systematic way. I agreed to be a discussant anyway but, in doing so, I felt . . . guilty. Or was it shame? "I'll have to look that up in Akhtar's (2009) *Comprehensive Dictionary of Psychoanalysis*," I thought. But then immediately I felt guilty—or was it shame?—for still getting confused about the distinction between guilt and shame after more than thirty years of psychoanalytic experience.

I took some comfort in knowing that it would be more than a year before I received the actual paper I would be discussing, so I would have plenty of time to develop some of my own ideas about guilt. But then every few weeks when I would tell myself that I really *should* start formulating and writing down my ideas, a curious thing would happen. Four ideas about guilt would come immediately to mind—the same four ideas each time. And then each time, I would have the same kind of uneasy guilty-shamey feeling that these were pretty lame ideas—they weren't even particularly psychoanalytic—and that someone with my level of training and experience should have something a lot more substantive and sophisticated to say about guilt than these ideas suggested. But then each time I would shrug off the guilty-shamey feeling, thinking, "At least they are a place to start. . . . I'll work on them later."

When I got to this point in composing the introduction to my discussion, I realized that I was feeling more comfortable than I would have expected about describing my uneasy feeling as "guilty-shamey." Although I had intended it as a self-deprecatingly humorous acknowledgment of my uncertainty about the difference between guilt and shame, it actually felt like an accurate description of the uneasy feeling I had repeatedly experienced, in which, on reflection, I could now clearly discern distinct elements of both guilt and shame. So it appeared that my guilty-shamey feeling had misled or intimidated me into believing that I was confused about guilt and shame when in fact I had understood the difference between them all along. Perhaps the guilty-shamey feeling had similarly misled and intimidated me into believing that my four ideas were psychoanalytically inadequate. Maybe they were actually important ideas.

It then occurred to me that I was writing about these four ideas in a way that was almost certain to pique my audience's curiosity. I imagined people eagerly wanting to hear my allegedly lame ideas, anticipating that they would turn out to be much more substantive than my guilty-shamey feeling had been telling me that they were. Everyone would be rooting for the undervalued ideas and thinking "Boooo!" to the guilty-shamey feeling. At this point, I realized that I was starring in my own *Rocky* fantasy, with the guilty-shamey feeling being some combination of Apollo Creed dancing rings around Rocky and Coach Mickey telling him that he's a bum for not doing more with his talent. "Hmmm. So who's my Apollo Creed in this scenario?" I mused. "Someone who makes me feel that I don't belong in the same intellectual ring with him? It must be Salman Akhtar, always so confident, knowledgeable and articulate about everything. . . . I sure hope it's not Stanley Coen. That would mean I'm unconsciously viewing this discussion as a fight. I'll have to watch out for signs of incompletely analyzed oedipal competitiveness as I write."

Well, actually those last two self-reflective thoughts were more like subliminal glimmers or proto-thoughts. The idea of an oedipal boxing match with my friend Stanley Coen was more uncomfortable than I was ready to dwell on at the time. So I slid past it and moved on to the other actor in my inner drama. "So who's the Coach Mickey who keeps getting on me about underperforming?" I wondered. "Oooh . . . Right . . . My father . . . The man who once said to me, 'Now that you're going off to Harvard, I have one piece of advice for you. Just try not to be such an ass as you were in high school.'"

What my father meant by being an ass was being complacent and self-satisfied, even cocky . . . like Apollo Creed, oddly enough. He wanted me to be more serious and disciplined and not kid myself that I could continue playing around and winging it all the time and expect to succeed just because I was smart. As it turned out he was partly right. My tendency to play around and wing it does sometimes turn me into a Disney's-Pinocchio kind of ass, ignoring my inner voice and losing myself in the superficial distractions and addictively competitive games of Pleasure Island (i.e., popular American culture). In that sense, my father's guilty-shamey advice—as I internalized it—could have the effect of calling me back to myself, encouraging me to take myself more seriously, to be true to what I really care about and work for something that really matters.

What my father didn't understand, however, is that I also have a strong tendency to be a Shakespeare's-Bottom-the-Weaver kind of ass, and that for me to succeed the way my father wanted me to, I would need to accept and embrace this ass-headed tendency in myself. I would need to learn that, for me, the tendency to play around and wing it also functions as a kind of introspective instinct that leads me to the inner space where I can be creative. It hasn't always been easy to trust this instinct—as in trusting that my four seemingly lame ideas will ultimately lead me where I need to go in this discussion—because I have *always* had that guilty-shamey feeling to remind me that I am being an ass. But eventually, I learned to take what was good in my father's advice and use it to enhance rather than stifle my instinct. I learned to become less complacent and more disciplined in the *way* I wing it, more serious about how I play around; as in free association and evenly hovering attention; and as in the way I am trying to write this discussion: going with the flow of consciousness while being assiduously attentive and reflective about it. Much like the method of systematic, disciplined but at the same time relaxed self-scanning that Stanley Coen describes and illustrates so well in his paper.

I consider Coen's method to be the heart and soul of psychoanalysis. Not only is it invaluable as a way to avoid getting caught up in harmful enactments. It is a model for the kind of inner and intersubjective listening that psychoanalysts should be practicing in every therapeutic hour, the kind of listening that gives us entry into the sacred space where healing can occur. It is to this space that Coen refers when he says to Mr. R, "Welcome to the playground of feelings."

PLAYGROUND OF FEELINGS AS SACRED SPACE: REFLECTIONS FROM SHAKESPEARE

In Shakespeare's *A Midsummer Night's Dream,* this sacred space of playing, feeling, and healing is represented by the woods in the moonlight, where the fairies have dominion. It is contrasted with the workaday city of Athens where Duke Theseus holds court. The city is a place of laws, ceremonies, politics, and linear logic, where life appears to be safe but really isn't, because actions can be destructive, and can have life-altering consequences. In contrast, the woods are a place of dreams, strong emotions, and non-linear connectedness where life appears to be frightening but really isn't, because actions are more like feelings—trial actions—that aren't dangerous because they can be undone and revised by the fairies.

Coen's message—metaphorically—is that if our inner attitude and approach keep the psychoanalytic process restricted to the city by day (where change is supposed to happen through interpretation and interpretations are arrived at through a logical thought process), then we will never get to the playground of feelings and we are at risk for doing serious harm to our patients. Using Coen's method, however, we can move the process into the more frightening but healing space of the woods by night, where change is an alteration of consciousness brought about by a deep emotional connection to both self and other that is felt by both patient and analyst. This is where Bottom-the-Ass comes in.

You may recall that in Shakespeare's play, Bottom is the central figure in the group of craftsmen and laborers who come to the woods (in Act I, scene ii) to rehearse a play for Duke Theseus's wedding celebration. Bottom immediately tries to take over the rehearsal. In his childishly self-important, self-satisfied but fundamentally lovable exuberance, Bottom eagerly volunteers to play every part in the play and tries to direct it too. Meanwhile, in the background, the fairy, Puck, observes Bottom's hubristic foolishness and gets the entertaining idea to literally make an ass out of him (transforming his head into that of an ass)—anticipating by almost 375 years my father's response to *my* hubristic foolishness. But Shakespeare understood something about Bottom that Puck and my father failed to appreciate: of all the characters in the play whose lives are unconsciously influenced, manipulated, even controlled, by the fairies, Bottom is the only character who actually gets to *see* the fairies, *and he must become an ass to do so.* Shakespeare seems to be suggesting that being an ass gives one access to a special realm of experience that is closed off to others. Bottom experiences his visit to this realm as a dream—a dream so compelling that he wakes from it with a feeling of awe and a need to capture his experience in words. In attempting to do so, he calls upon the words of a sacred text (Paul 1 Corinthians 2:9) which he garbles in a uniquely Bottom-like way that paradoxically manages to heighten the sense of the sacred:

> I have had a most rare vision. I have had a dream, past the wit of man to say what dream it was. Man is but an ass, if he go about to expound this dream. Methought I was—there is no man can tell what. Methought I was,—and methought I had,—but man is but a patched fool, if he will offer to say what methought I had. The eye of man hath not heard, the ear of man hath not seen, man's hand is not able to taste, his tongue to conceive, nor his heart to report, what my dream was. I will get Peter Quince to write a ballad of this dream: it shall be called Bottom's Dream, because it hath no bottom. [IV.i.203-215]

I admit that I have, on several occasions, had just this kind of bottomless experience of wholeness during a psychoanalytic hour, when a new understanding has emerged in a moment of deep simultaneous connection to myself and to my patient. This is the kind of profoundly private but simultaneously intersubjective experience that Thomas Ogden (1994) so beautifully described in his seminal paper on "the analytic third." And it is the kind of experience Stanley Coen describes with Mr. R, that moved him to say (with Bottom-like exuberance), "Welcome to the playground of feelings" and that moved Mr. R (newly brought to life) to say, "I want more."

The point I take from Shakespeare is that to enter the realm of the fairies, the playground of feelings, the sacred space where healing happens, psychoanalysts have to be a bit like Bottom. We need a kind of naive, primitive but innocent, narcissistic vitality that makes us want to play every part in the drama of life. Through the introspective/empathic experience of countertransference and transference, we get to do just that. Our introspective/empathic awareness of our inner and intersubjective life moves the psychoanalytic process into the woods and gives us access to a special realm of experience to which most people, most of the time, are closed off.

The point I take from Stanley Coen is much the same. The method of psychoanalytic listening and self-scanning that Coen advocates shows us the way into the woods. Like Bottom the Weaver, it is accepting of and fascinated by everything human, playful in the best Winnicottian (1971) sense of the term and at the same time *guided by a deeply moral sensibility*. I realize that on a superficial reading of *A Midsummer Night's Dream* it might not be apparent that moral sensibility is one of Bottom's more notable attributes. In fact, it wasn't apparent to me until I began to write this paragraph. Until then I had thought of Shakespeare's play as his poetic commentary on creativity. I now see it, in addition, as a dramatic commentary on morality, with Bottom the Weaver as the play's moral center. When told he is to play the character of Pyramus in the play before the Duke, Bottom asks a simple but profoundly important moral question around which the entire play revolves:

What is Pyramus? A lover or a tyrant? [I.ii.19]

This question applies with great immediacy to all twelve major characters in *A Midsummer Night's Dream*, each of whom at some point behaves tyrannically toward one or more of the others, and does so *ostensibly in the name of love*. So, just as Shakespeare intended *A Midsummer Night's Dream* to be a commentary on the vicissitudes of human love, I believe he intended Bottom's question to be a commentary on the moral ambiguity—the knowledge of good and evil—that is inherent in the experience of human love, and to the moral choices this entails.

COEN'S SELF-SCANNING AND THE KNOWLEDGE OF GOOD AND EVIL

It is precisely these moral choices to which Stanley Coen calls our attention in his discussion of sexual boundary violations and other harms that psychoanalysts can do to patients. Coen's method of superego-informed self-scanning is a way for us to apply Bottom's question to ourselves: are we lovers, compassionately acting in our patient's best interests, or are we tyrants, taking advantage of the power we have over patients to use them for our own interests? Considering the disturbingly high incidence of sexual boundary violations among psychoanalysts, it is apparent that too many of us never stop to ask ourselves this question. We don't do the kind of superego-informed self-scanning that Stanley Coen recommends or we don't do it regularly and systematically enough. We remain oblivious to the deeper emotional undercurrents in our moment-to-moment interaction with patients because we are afraid to feel and take responsibility for certain dark and disturbing emotions in ourselves. The inevitable result is that, instead of accepting and allowing ourselves to feel these emotions, we unreflectively act on them, often harming our patients in the process. At a time when the future of psychoanalysis hangs in the balance, this kind of bad faith practice is hardly conducive to our survival as a profession.

Stanley Coen teaches us how to practice psychoanalysis in good faith: first, doing no harm to our patients, and second, helping them to heal. Coen's method of self-scanning is an instruction manual for how to embody in our work the core value of psychoanalysis—to maintain an accepting, non-judgmental but morally discerning introspective and empathic awareness of ourselves and our patients—a value famously crystallized in the aphorism of Terence: "I am a human and I count nothing human as foreign to me." As Coen puts it:

> A tolerant, loving attitude toward the analyst's affective experience enables him to help his patient to tolerate, and then to modify and resolve, conflict. This tolerant attitude can apply to what the analyst fears and hates in himself but needs to bear, in himself and in his patient, for the sake of this patient's treatment. (p. 70)

Coen invites us to apply this attitude by imagining ourselves not just in the shoes but in the bodies and minds of both lover and tyrant, both victim and victimizer, both betrayed and betrayer, because the capacity and the tendency to treat each other in all of these ways surely exist both in our patients and in ourselves. This means embracing the Bottom in all of us, our desire to experience fully every part in our own life drama and in our patients' dramas. But it also means accepting the darker, shadow side of Bottom's hubristic exuberance, the lustful, murderous creature in us that has the body of a man and the head not of an ass but of a bull, the

Minotaur. This frightening image is a subtle but important undercurrent in *A Midsummer Night's Dream*. Shakespeare evokes it partly by showing the Minotaur's comic parallel in Bottom, partly by showing how easily lovers can become tyrants, and partly by having Bottom perform his play for Theseus, the same mythological hero who killed the Minotaur in the labyrinth of Crete but then went on to betray the love of both Ariadne and Hippolyta.

The point is that healing—*making whole*—requires accepting and integrating the disturbing disowned parts of ourselves—the ass Bottom, the tyrant Minotaur, and the betrayer Theseus—so that we can then accept and help our patients accept these disowned parts of themselves. Coen describes how this process of acceptance happened in his work with Mr. R; how he needed to feel and accept in himself his rage at Mr. R, his wish to get rid of him, even a wish that Mr. R kill himself. Only then could Coen begin to understand that, in wanting to get rid of Mr. R, he was wanting to get rid of the disturbing feelings that Mr. R was provoking in him. In fact, Mr. R's relentlessly provocative behavior—forcing Coen to worry about Mr. R's safety while missing sessions and responding negatively to Coen's efforts to help—expressed a desire to be pursued and fucked, not only in anger but more importantly out of love. To appreciate this, Coen first needed to feel how his rage at Mr. R contained not only the disturbing countertransference to get rid of him but an equally disturbing desire to 'come after him,' aggressively, wanting to break down his enraging passive-aggressive defenses, and force Mr. R to open himself up to the help that Coen was trying to give him. This deepened awareness helped Coen become more comfortable with his own anger, because he could now feel that it embodied not only a destructive but a loving impulse that was responsive to Mr. R's passive wishes. Coen's more relaxed accepting attitude then allowed Mr. R to become more engaged in treatment. He began to talk about his desire to be penetrated anally. This, in turn, allowed Coen to feel the sexual element in his countertransference wish to pursue and break through to Mr. R. Only then could he appreciate that being fucked is not only being tyrannized but being loved, and that being a fucker is also being a lover. "Welcome to the playground of feelings."

Coen's account, as I read it, implies that to enter the playground of feelings requires a loving acceptance of self and other that can happen only through confronting our inner demons, allowing ourselves to fully experience our most disturbing emotions, understand them, and accept them as part of ourselves and of our patients. This *should* be a common experience in psychoanalytic work, but it is rarely discussed in our literature, perhaps because we are embarrassed to admit how much our darker emotional impulses can intrude themselves into our work, but perhaps also because we are embarrassed to talk about the Bottom-like enthusiasm we feel when the process of experiencing and accepting our disturbing emotions leads to moments of deep connection with our patients, like the connection with Mr. R that Coen described as "we were 'on' with each other." To someone who hasn't experienced it, this kind of connection could sound like something that might *promote* boundary violations rather than prevent them. But in actual clinical practice, such a connection—arising out of an honest and thorough self-analysis of disturbing countertransference impulses—always entails increased compassion, never increased desire. I know this from my own clinical experience, but it is also a natural consequence of a guiding moral principle that Coen repeatedly emphasizes: Psychoanalysts do this kind of ongoing moment-to-moment exploration of our own disturbing emotions primarily *for the sake of the patient*, so that our own needs and desires don't get in the way of our understanding the patient's needs and desires.

I would add that it is impossible to come to an awareness of the inner and intersubjective life as a joyful playground of feelings without recognizing—as Bottom did—that this playground is a sacred space. It is the same inner and intersubjective play space that Winnicott described between child and mother, the creative space in which the spontaneous autonomous True Self is born (Winnicott, 1960, 1971). To hold this space sacred is an act of love. To ignore or violate it is an act of tyranny. Which brings me back to guilt, the topic from which I was diverted into an extended *Midsummer Night's* tangent by my father's internalized voice telling me not to be such an ass. By now, the reader has probably forgotten how curious you were a few pages ago to hear about my four lame ideas. That's OK. I'll tell you anyway.

FOUR IDEAS ABOUT GUILT

The first idea is a clinical impression I've developed in recent years that the guilt many of my patients experience is like a toxic foreign body, the internalization of parental attitudes that were in fact frighteningly hostile, often covertly, and were toxic to the point of soul murder. The highly narcissistic parents who induce this kind of soul-crushing guilt cannot tolerate, let alone appreciate, their child's unique individuality. They systematically violate the sacred play space between parent and child, invalidating or punishing any spontaneous gesture of the child's True Self, making them feel guilty and ashamed about what is most alive in them, as if any genuine self-expression is an offense punishable by death or shunning. The toxic foreign body type of superego that results from this emotional abuse is responsible for the most extreme form of the negative therapeutic reaction. It produces an almost knee-jerk reactivity in the patient that takes any sign of therapeutic progress as a capital offense and, much like the intolerant parent, viciously attacks or enviously undermines the patient for showing any sign of independent life, any tendency to thrive and grow outside the parental orbit.

I'm not talking about projection here. I'm talking about real parents doing real and devastating harm to their children so that the victimized children feel incapacitating guilt while the parents typically feel no guilt whatsoever. Of course, there is some degree of this kind of narcissism, this intolerance of otherness, in every parent—witness my father's intolerance of my 'ass-headedness'—and it leads to some degree of intolerance in the superego of every child. But the parent's narcissism is usually limited and is significantly mitigated by his genuine love for his child, which also becomes part of the child's superego, giving the child room to grow and thrive. Nevertheless, it is important to recognize that the most malignant and unmitigated form of soul-murdering narcissism is far from rare, not in parents, not in priests, and not in psychoanalysts.

The second and third of my lame ideas came from my Catholic-schooling but have stayed with me because they feel exactly right. One is the Golden Rule of empathy and mutuality: Do unto others as you would have others do unto you. There's also the Jewish version, from Rabbi Hillel: "That which is hateful to you, do not do to your neighbor. This is the whole Torah; the rest is commentary. Go and study it." The other idea from Catholicism is that there are two kinds of contrition: imperfect contrition, where guilt is primarily a fear of Hell, and perfect contrition, where guilt is primarily a feeling of remorse for hurting someone you love, namely God. And finally my fourth idea is a very similar distinction that Martin Buber made between two kinds of guilt: neurotic and authentic. Neurotic guilt is based on fear of being punished for transgressing parental and social taboos. It is an arbitrary, socially constructed guilt, where there may or may not be any basis in reality for feeling guilty. Authentic guilt is based in the reality of doing something that we know to be truly immoral; in Buber's words, "when someone injures an order of the human world whose foundations he knows and recognizes as those of his own existence and of all common human existence" (1957, p. 117).

Buber's language is notoriously allusive and poetical so it is difficult to be sure precisely what he means by this 'order of the human world' that is the foundation for our individual and common human existence. In terms of the Golden Rule of empathy and mutuality, I would say that Buber is referring to an innate moral sense through which we can *know* in every situation how to treat the other person because we can *know* how we would want to be treated in the same situation. But I am fairly certain that Buber means more specifically the underlying order of the human world that makes it possible for us to say I-Thou to each other. Here is one of Buber's many attempts to describe the essence of an I-Thou relationship, as contrasted with an I-It relationship:

> To be aware of a man . . . means in particular to perceive his wholeness
> as a person determined by the spirit; it means to perceive the dynamic
> center which stamps his every utterance, action, and attitude with the
> recognizable sign of uniqueness. Such an awareness is impossible,
> however, if and so long as the other is the separated object of my
> contemplation or even observation [i.e., as long as I am in an I-It rela-
> tion to the other], for this wholeness and its center do not let them-
> selves be known to contemplation or observation. It is only possible
> when I step into an elemental relation with the other—that is, when he
> becomes present to me. Hence I designate awareness in the special
> sense as "personal making present."(1957, p. 109)

I believe that the feeling awareness of self and other to which Coen as-
pires in his self-reflective method of psychoanalytic listening is just what
Buber meant by his concept of 'personal making present.' Authentic
guilt, in this context, would be the natural response to treating another
person in a way that hinders or prevents him from 'becoming' present;
that ignores, denies, or injures the possibility of wholeness inherent in his
unique personhood.

In a series of lectures to psychiatrists, Buber (1957) explained this in
terms of two basic but antithetical patterns of human relatedness—'imposing oneself on someone' versus 'helping someone to unfold'—which
he related to Kant's categorical imperative that one's fellow man must
never be thought of and treated merely as a means, but always at the
same time as an independent end.

There are two basic ways of affecting men in their views and their
attitude to life. In the first, a man tries to impose himself, his opinion and
his attitude, on the other. In the second, a man wishes to find and to
further in the soul of the other the disposition toward what he has recognized in himself as the right. The first way has been most powerfully
developed in the realm of propaganda, the second in that of education.

> The propagandist I have in mind, who imposes himself, is not in the
> least concerned with the person whom he desires to influence, as a
> person; various individual qualities are of importance only in so far as
> he can exploit them to win the other and must get to know them for
> this purpose.
>
> The educator whom I have in mind lives in a world of individuals,
> a certain number of whom are always at any one time committed to his
> care. He sees each of these individuals as in a position to become a
> unique, single person, and thus the bearer of a special task of existence
> which can be fulfilled through him and through him alone. He sees
> every personal life as engaged in such a process of actualization, and he
> knows from his own experience that the forces making for actualiza-
> tion are all the time involved in a microcosmic struggle with counter-
> forces. He has come to see himself as a helper of the actualizing
> forces. . . . He cannot wish to impose himself, for he believes in the
> effect of the actualizing forces—that is, he believes that in every man

what is right is established in a single and uniquely personal way.
(1957, p. 110-111)

In this distinction between 'imposing oneself on someone' and 'helping someone to unfold,' the imposing-on implies and expresses an 'I-It' attitude, a position of detachment from which I see and treat the other as an objectified person completely separate from me. This is a natural and necessary way for humans to see each other, according to Buber, and becomes problematic only when it is not balanced by an 'I-Thou' appreciation of the other as a unique individual like ourselves, to whom we feel connected in the mutuality of our human becoming. In this problematic case—having an exclusively I-It attitude unbalanced by any I-Thou awareness—we will naturally tend to impose ourselves on the other, exploiting him or her as a narcissistic object.

Frank Summers (2001) discusses the same ideas in Winnicottian terms. He argues that the models of therapeutic action currently accepted in different schools of psychoanalytic thought—interpretation and insight, internalization of the analyst's self-psychological functions, or the impact of the real relationship with a collaborative co-constructing analyst—all emphasize in one way or another what the (active) analyst must do or provide for the (passive) patient, and all fail to appreciate that the healing process is internally generated by the patient. In Buber's terms, they all entail the analyst being in an I-It relation to the patient, in which he doesn't recognize the patient's dynamic center and his innate tendency toward self-unfolding and actualization. The alternative Winnicottian model that Summers recommends is very reminiscent of Buber's account of the ideal I-Thou educator.

> The analyst's task is to be alert to the importance of the patient's spontaneous gesture and respond in a way that facilitates rather than impinges on it. Often the patient's true self-expressions remain undeveloped because the analyst does not see their potentially decisive importance. Just as the child needs the parental figure to see and nurture inborn capacities, the patient needs an analyst who will engage his or her efforts to develop in a new direction. At this point, the clinical strategy is not provision of insight or functions, nor even emotional relating, but a kind of midwifery that recognizes the emerging material as a potential authentic expression of unrealized aspects of the self. The analytic task is both to see the emerging true self in the patient's anxiety-free interests, thoughts, desires, and affects, and to aid their development into new, more authentic ways of being and relating.

In a similar vein, Hoffman (2004) describes Winnicott's true self as "a silent wellspring of creative and authentic living . . . that . . . produces an innate inclination toward maturation"—terms very reminiscent of Buber's idea of an innate authentic direction that unfolds naturally from the dynamic center of the individual when facilitated by an I-Thou educator. Hoffman quotes Winnicott's observation that

> In each baby is a vital spark, and this urge towards life and growth and development is . . . something the child is born with and which is carried forward in a way that we do not have to understand . . . You do not have to make the bulb grow into a daffodil. You supply the right kind of earth or fibre and you keep the bulb watered just the right amount, and the rest comes naturally, because the bulb has life in it.

If we review Stanley Coen's interaction with Mr. R in light of these ideas, we could say that in becoming aware and accepting of his own disturbing emotional reactions to Mr. R, Coen became able not only to see Mr. R's pathology (an I-It stance) but to see through the pathology to an I-Thou recognition of 'the emerging true self' that was unfolding even in Mr. R's apparently regressive desire to be anally penetrated by a dominatrix.

THE MORALITY OF STANLEY COEN'S SUPEREGO

Putting together some of the main ideas I have discussed so far, I would propose that there is an energy of both love (I-Thou mutual unfolding) and tyranny (I-It imposing) in every impulse of the human heart. The Golden Rule tells us that we should recognize both energies in ourselves and choose to do the right—more loving and unfolding, less tyrannical and imposing—thing. Stanley Coen tells us how to put this Golden Rule into practice with our patients. His message, in summary, is that we are all motivated to serve the best interests of the patient—in Buber's terms, to facilitate their unfolding and actualization—but at the same time we also have unconscious impulses to misuse patients for our own interests (in Buber's terms imposing ourselves on them). In order to do right by our patients and to avoid misusing and harming them, we need to scan our moment-to-moment inner experience for derivatives of these problematic unconscious impulses. The scanning involves listening for the signals we get from our superego when unconscious needs and desires to impose on patients become activated in us. In so doing, we can become aware of these potentially destructive needs and desires, accept them and learn from them, using them to understand ourselves and the patient so that we can restrain ourselves from acting on them and instead choose an approach that serves the best interests of the patient. We may not always get to the playground of feelings, but we can at least stay in that neighborhood.

That's the summary. Here's the catch: In order to do this superego-informed self-scanning, an analyst would need to have precisely the kind of superego that Coen describes: a superego that oversees, guides, criticizes, restrains, praises, and loves; and moreover a superego that is motivated by love, respect, and compassion for the patient and for ourselves.

Unfortunately, not all analysts have this kind of loving, guiding super-ego; and those who do may not recognize it, since it bears so little resemblance to the superego as Freud defined it, the product of internalized parental and societal prohibitions. People who are motivated by Freud's kind of superego are not being overseen and guided by a compassionate inner observer. Rather, they are being monitored by an instinctive agency that automatically punishes them with guilt feelings (which I would now say are more accurately described as *guilty-shamey* feelings) whenever their temptations or their actions trigger one or more of the primal fears: fear of castration or other retaliation; fear of loss of love or respect; fear of abandonment or ostracism; or, as in the toxic foreign body kind of guilt I described earlier, fear of annihilation or soul-murder. An analyst motivated by Freud's kind of superego would restrain himself from violating sexual boundaries not out of empathy and respect for the patient, but out of fear of what might happen to him if he did what he wanted. He wouldn't have clear inner knowledge that it is always wrong to have sex with a patient. He would know only that it is forbidden.

At this point I can begin to recognize the direction of my own personal unfolding in a line of thought that now emerges from my four 'lame' ideas. I feel validated in having trusted these ideas because, if we put them together with Stanley Coen's ideas, they lead to the interesting proposition that there are two kinds of superego, Freud's and Coen's. One generates neurotic, socially constructed guilt and imperfect contrition out of fear of getting caught and punished; the other generates authentic existential guilt and perfect contrition or *remorse* out of a desire to treat others with love, respect, and compassion. Freud's superego, although we do participate in its construction, remains like a foreign body or external voice in our heads that becomes part of our Winnicottian False Self. Coen's superego is like a higher consciousness that has knowledge of good and evil and serves as the moral compass of our True Self. I should point out that Coen actually includes *both* of these superegos in his account of psychoanalytic self-scanning. There is Freud's internalized superego agency automatically generating what Coen calls superego signals and then there is Coen's overseeing, compassionate inner presence recognizing and using these signals self-reflectively, to restrain us from doing the wrong thing and guide us toward doing the right thing.

SUPEREGO AS HIGHER CONSCIOUSNESS: THE CONTRIBUTION OF ROBERT WAELDER

I know that many analysts will object to the spiritual implications of my describing Coen's superego as a 'higher consciousness.' I do so because I want to highlight the fact that Coen's superego—as he describes it—has an autonomous moral awareness and discernment that clearly puts it in a different category from the Freudian superego that we all know and fear. It is worth considering where Coen could have gotten this idea of a superego that is so different from Freud's. It bears some resemblance to Roy Schafer's (1960) 'loving and beloved superego,' but Schafer's super- ego is really only slightly different from Freud's. It is still produced by a socially constructed internalization of parental and societal attitudes, only they are positive attitudes rather than punitive ones. Coen's super- ego is much more than that. It may be informed by such internalized positive attitudes — like Leo Stone's humanizing voice in Coen's head — but it functions as an autonomous, morally discerning mind of its own that integrates positive and punitive attitudes from without with its own independent attitudes and values from within.

To me, Coen's superego sounds more like that described by Robert Waelder (1930) in his paper on 'the principle of multiple function':

> The superego . . . is the element by which man . . . goes beyond himself, taking himself as an object, whether acting in a punishing aggressive way, or lovingly caring, or . . . being disinterestedly objective, as in self-observation and the ability to depart from his own point of view . . . not only experiencing the world around one in its momentary relationship to one's drives and interests, but also . . . recognizing its existence apart from one's own ego. . . . (I)t is the superego which distinguishes the nature of man from that of animals. (pp. 82-83)

Years later, Waelder wrote that "The ability to step back and take a look at oneself from an imaginary observation point — the self-consciousness or the transcendence of one's self as it has been called by philosophers . . . is the essence of the superego function" (1965, p. 59). There's nothing socially constructed there, no internalization of parental or societal atti- tudes. Just a higher consciousness that transcends, observes, loves, criti- cizes, and guides the self.

In calling to mind Waelder's superego, I suddenly realize that I *have* thought about guilt before, and have even written about it several times (Frattaroli 1990, 2001, 2008). So it seems that my guilty-shamey feeling had a more powerful impact on me than I had imagined. It intimidated me into forgetting my previous work on the subject of guilt and con- vinced me, temporarily at least, that I really didn't have much to say about it. Clearly this was my Freudian superego, the internalized voice of my father, trying to make sure I don't get too cocky.

As I have discussed elsewhere (2001), Waelder's superego integrated Freud's earliest ideas about the ego ideal, self-observation, and con- science from his paper on narcissism (1914b) with what he later called the superego in *The Ego and the Id* (1923). I have argued that, just as Freud's term '*das Ich*' is best translated not as 'the ego,' but as 'the I,' so, too, Waelder's superego concept suggests a more accurate translation for Freud's '*das Überich,*' not as 'the superego' but as 'the I that stands above.'

Waelder didn't want to draw attention to what such a translation would highlight, however—the element of transcendence (higher consciousness) in his reconceptualization of the superego. He knew that Freud could never have accepted such an idea. Freud was uneasy about the unscientifically spiritual implications of the detached, self-reflective, morally evaluating consciousness he had begun to describe in 1914, so he had limited the focus of his later discussions to superego as internalized prohibitions, a concept more easily explainable in the quasi-neurological terms of his libido theory. But in limiting himself to what he thought could be explained scientifically, Freud was forced to leave out of his account of human nature the single most distinctive feature of human experience, the higher consciousness that gives us our capacity for self-reflection, objective observation, compassion, and morality.

Like Waelder in 1930, Coen has put back into Freud's theory this higher consciousness that Freud left out, and has amplified Waelder's description by emphasizing its moral dimension: our capacity to distinguish and choose between right and wrong in putting the patient's interests before our own. But having described this overseeing, guiding, compassionately accepting but restraining, self-reflective, moral consciousness, and having called it the superego, Coen too, like Waelder, omits comment on how and why it is different from Freud's superego. Unlike Waelder, Coen didn't have Freud personally looking over his shoulder. But he may nevertheless have been inhibited by Freud's prejudice against any idea that sounds too spiritual. This prejudice is part of an institutional foreign-body superego that all psychoanalysts internalize through their training and socialization as psychoanalysts. As evidence, I would ask the reader to consider your reactions to my use of the terms 'sacred' and 'higher consciousness' in this article and to my discussion of Buber's moral philosophy. I suspect that most readers were entirely comfortable with Coen's description of the superego *until* I suggested that he was actually describing a higher moral consciousness (which would suggest further that our clinical practice of psychoanalysis—whether and how we use Coen's method of self-scanning—inevitably expresses our underlying moral philosophy).

So where did Coen get such an un-Freudian idea? Probably not from Waelder, who so understated his radical departure from Freud that not even Freud himself noticed. Even in the psychoanalytic literature since Freud, I could find only three writers (Klein, 1976; Frattaroli, 1990, 2001; Friedman, 2007) who have recognized that Waelder's multiple function paper constituted a radical revision of Freud's entire structural theory. So it seems more likely that Coen got his concept of the superego not from Waelder, but from the same place Waelder got it, which is also the place from which we his readers can all immediately understand the idea; namely, from his/our own self-reflection, from recognizing within ourselves the consciousness that can observe our passions dispassionately, that can hear the punitive voice of our Freudian superego but listen to it compassionately, and that can use its signals to understand what is happening in the clinical moment and to sort out what response would best serve the needs of the patient.

THE LACK OF MORALITY IN FREUD'S THEORY AND PRACTICE: THE CASE OF DORA REVISITED

In highlighting the fact that Coen's and Waelder's superego represents a higher moral consciousness, an 'I that stands above,' that is nowhere to be found in Freudian theory, I know I risk making everyone, including Stanley Coen himself, uncomfortable. I do so because I believe there are dangerous consequences for psychoanalysis from having a theory that leaves out this higher consciousness *and its guiding moral compass*. Coen had to formulate his own concept of a superego that knows it is morally wrong to misuse patients, because there is no such faculty of moral awareness in Freud's theory. It is a disturbing fact that nowhere in his writings does Freud suggest that it is morally wrong or even psychologically unhealthy to selfishly use other people for one's own sexual gratification. Quite the contrary, his theory suggests that this is the most basic human tendency and that its frustration by the demands of civilization is one of the causes of mental illness. Even in his early writings about patients who had been sexually abused by their fathers, Freud's idea of what was traumatic and pathogenic about the abuse was *not* that it was a heinous violation of the child's nascent personhood and a betrayal of the sacred trust between parent and child, but merely that it entailed a premature overstimulation of the child's sexual drive. That's why it was called seduction and not abuse. Morality had nothing to do with it.

Unfortunately, the amorality of the seduction theory is far from the most damaging consequence of Freud's failure to include morality in his thinking about human nature. Generations of analysts have practiced psychoanalysis in a way that unwittingly ignored the wholeness and uniqueness of their patients and instead imposed on them a pathologizing reductionistic theory of human nature to which the patients were expected to conform. And Freud himself was the avatar of this *immoral* (tyrannical, I-It imposing rather than loving, I-Thou unfolding) style of psychoanalytic practice. After rejecting the seduction theory, Freud, in his zeal to advance his new sexual theory of neurosis, proceeded to impose this theory on his patient Dora, exploiting her for his own ideological purposes, much in the style of Buber's extreme propagandist. In the process, he both condoned and symbolically perpetrated a traumatic sexual boundary violation whose obvious immorality he quite stunningly failed to recognize.

Eighteen-year-old Dora told Freud that when she was fourteen, Herr K, a family friend who had known Dora for years and treated her like a daughter, had suddenly tried to force himself on her sexually. When Dora subsequently learned that Frau K, (with whom Dora had been very close) had been having a clandestine affair with Dora's father, she realized that "she had been handed over to Herr K. as the price of his tolerating the relations between her father and his wife" (Freud, 1905, p. 34). Moreover, Dora had become symptomatic after telling her father about Herr K's second attempt to seduce her when she was sixteen, only to have her father believe Herr K's protestations that he had done nothing improper and that Dora must have *imagined* his advances because—as Frau K had told him—Dora was interested in nothing but sex.

Shockingly, Freud believed all these details of Dora's account and yet seemed to have no awareness that anything immoral was being done to her, nor did he have any suspicion that her symptoms might be connected to the fact that three adults she had loved, trusted, and depended on had, first, betrayed her; second, denied that any betrayal had happened; and third, gaslighted her by impugning her character for having imagined such a thing. Quite the contrary, Freud compounded the betrayal *and* the gaslighting by quite forcibly trying to convince Dora that she had really wanted Herr K's advances all along, and that it would have been to everyone's benefit had she married him as she (according to Freud) had really wanted to do, instead of rejecting him and becoming neurotic as a result.

Before rereading the Dora case for purposes of this discussion, I hadn't recognized how egregiously Freud had misused his patient. I had been taught as a candidate in the late 1970s that Dora was a landmark case in which Freud discovered (too late) the power of the transference. Although I did notice that Freud had taken everything Dora said and used it to prove his preconceived theory, I took the lead from my teachers in believing that, since his theory was valid, his therapeutic end more or less justified his overbearingly suggestive means. Reading the case now, however, I find Freud's attitude and behavior toward Dora nothing less than inexcusable. Here is a quote that illustrates why (in the italicized sentences):

> She was fourteen years old at the time. Herr K. had made an arrangement with her and his wife that they should meet him one afternoon at his place of business in the principal square of B—so as to have a view of a church festival. He persuaded his wife, however, to stay at home, and sent away his clerks, so that he was alone when the girl arrived. When the time for the procession approached, he asked the girl to wait for him at the door which opened on to the staircase leading to the upper story, while he pulled down the outside shutters. He then came back, and, instead of going out by the open door, suddenly clasped the girl to him and pressed a kiss upon her lips. *This was surely just the*

situation to call up a distinct feeling of sexual excitement in a girl of fourteen who had never before been approached. But Dora had at that moment a violent feeling of disgust, tore herself free from the man, and hurried past him to the staircase and from there to the street door. In this scene, *the behaviour of this child of fourteen was already entirely and completely hysterical. I should without question consider a person hysterical in whom an occasion for sexual excitement elicited feelings that were preponderantly or exclusively unpleasurable*; and I should do so whether or not the person were capable of producing somatic symptoms. The elucidation of the mechanism of this reversal of affect is one of the most important and at the same time one of the most difficult problems in the psychology of the neuroses [my italics].

To appreciate the self-serving, cavalier presumptuousness of the argument Freud so relentlessly tried to force on Dora, consider that the 'reversal of affect' logic he applied to Dora's feeling of disgust is tantamount to insisting that any hungry person who is unexpectedly disgusted by the taste of tainted food must secretly have been yearning to be poisoned.

Freud could never have so badly mishandled Dora's treatment had he listened to her *and to himself* with the self-aware moral sensibility of Stanley Coen's superego. The fact is, Dora fled treatment not, as Freud speculated, because he had failed to recognized her transference soon enough, but because he failed to recognize and respect her dignity and value as a person. He acknowledged but then rationalized away the truth that Herr K, Frau K, and Dora's own father had violated both her sexual and psychological boundaries. He failed either to recognize or to take seriously that their treatment of Dora was immoral and psychologically destructive—*whether or not* Dora had ever been secretly in love with Herr K *or* her father. Similarly Freud failed to recognize that he himself had demonstrated the same immoral disregard for Dora's psychological well-being, treating her as a sex object to be used for his own purposes. Where Herr K had tried to force her to submit to his sexual desire, Freud tried to force her to submit to his sexual interpretations. No wonder Dora fled from both men.

So if Freud never recognized the immorality of a parent sexually abusing his own child, if he failed to recognize the immorality of his own self-serving misuse of Dora—as is evident from his lack of guilt or shame in publishing the details of how he understood and treated her—how then can we expect psychoanalysts who have been trained in the Freudian tradition to recognize the immorality of an analyst having sex with a patient, not to mention the immorality of more subtle misuses of our patients? This is not a rhetorical question. Generations of psychoanalytic candidates have been taught, as I was, that Freud's Dora case is a model of proper psychoanalytic thinking and practice. Many of us have unquestioningly followed this model to the great detriment of our patients. We may think we know better now, but I doubt that there is a single psychoanalytic institute that currently teaches the Dora case for what it really is: a cautionary model of what psychoanalysis *at its worst* can be.

SELF-REFLECTION: PSYCHOANALYSIS WITH AND WITHOUT MORALITY

What would it take for us to transcend our institutional repetition compulsion and stop internalizing and perpetuating Freud's most misguided attitudes? I submit that it would require a significant change in our psychoanalytic culture. We would first need to acknowledge that morality (not just ethics) *matters*. This in turn would require us to acknowledge that we do have a higher moral consciousness—the consciousness that is capable of an I-Thou awareness—through which we can discern the difference between right and wrong, love and tyranny, unfolding from within and imposition from without, acting in the best interests of another person versus misusing another person to serve our own interests. It would then have to become a standard of psychoanalytic teaching and practice that we use this higher consciousness on an ongoing basis to do the kind of self-scanning that Stanley Coen recommends.

When I follow Coen's suggestion and try to put myself in the heart and mind-set of an analyst who has sex with a patient, imagining possible circumstances under which I might do the same thing myself, my first thought is that I consider the analyst-patient relationship, like the parent-child relationship, to be a sacred trust, and I would consider any sexual boundary violation to be a betrayal of that trust. My second thought is that I cannot honestly imagine that I could ever violate a patient's trust so flagrantly unless my higher consciousness were completely out of commission—for example, due to early Alzheimer's, medication side effect, or other neurological impairment. Otherwise, I would become consciously aware, as soon as I became aroused, that I was in danger of doing something that would be destructive to my patient as a person and destructive to any possibility that I could be therapeutically helpful to her. Knowing that this would be both immoral and unethical, I simply wouldn't do it. Not that I couldn't be tempted. I can imagine that, if my personal life were in shambles, I could became vulnerable to believing the transference projection of a very attractive patient who believed that I was her soul mate and could get caught up in a countertransference infatuation of my own. Or in a similar situation, I could imagine being sexually tantalized simply by knowing that I could now have my way with a captivating woman who would be unobtainable to me were she not my patient. But in these situations, I cannot imagine being able to forget, rationalize, or not care about the immoral destructiveness of what I was tempted to do. I could get carried away in fantasy only so far and then would be brought up short—my higher consciousness would be re-

awakened and I would be prompted to stop and reflect—by the stum-
bling block of my erection.

To put it in the simplest terms, I couldn't have sex with a patient
without being sexually aroused and I couldn't become sexually aroused
without knowing that I was aroused, and I couldn't know that I was
aroused without feeling both alarmed and curious about it. Alarmed because I would know that my arousal constituted a destructive desire to
set aside my patient's therapeutic needs—needs which I have a sacred
obligation to serve—so that I could misuse her for my own sexual gratification. Curious because I would know that some defensive purpose was
being served for both my patient and myself by this dramatic sexualiza-
tion of our analytic relationship. So however much I might be tempted to
act or speak in the heat of my aroused desire, I would feel both morally
and professionally obligated to deal with my arousal analytically, taking
it as a cue to stop and reflect on what was happening between me and the
patient in that moment. I would know—as a general principle that applies whenever the analyst becomes aware that he is in the grip of any
strong emotion—that I should refrain from saying or doing anything
until I had self-reflectively sorted out what had triggered my arousal and
until I understood the triggers well enough that I could shift my focus
from my own desire to an empathic awareness of what the patient actually needed from me in that moment, which would never be sexual.

Again, I'm not saying that I could never become sexually aroused in a
session or that my higher consciousness is never asleep. Like all analysts,
I do fall into unconscious enactments with patients quite frequently in
which my higher consciousness doesn't wake up and alert me until after
the fact. For me, this usually involves some degree of feeling frustrated
and helpless and impatient because I'm having trouble making emotional
contact with a patient who is in pain, so that I feel the patient to be in
some way inaccessible to my therapeutic efforts. The harmful countertransference reaction I am most vulnerable to in these situations is to
become intolerant of the patient's pain or of my own helplessness. At
times, my tendency is to counteract my feeling of helplessness by losing
interest in what the patient is saying and getting lost in my own train of
thought. At other times my tendency is to counteract the patient's pain by
becoming overly invested in finding something therapeutic to say to relieve the pain, what Freud called *furor sanandi*—the rage to cure. But I can
also imagine this kind of countertransference frustration leading me to
fantasize about trying to get through to the patient sexually. I can even
imagine fantasizing that this might be therapeutic for the patient. And if
there were other things going on in my life that were making me feel
ineffectual, needy, and helpless, I can imagine such a fantasy becoming
very compelling indeed. But by the time I had an erection I am confident
that I would be alarmed and curious enough to recognize that I was in
the grip of a harmful countertransference reaction in which any story I

was telling myself that sex might be beneficial to the patient could only be a sleazy rationalization. Even if I had a strong feeling that I was in love with the patient, I would know that this feeling involved a significant component of needing something emotionally from the patient and I would know that to use a patient in this way would be to betray the patient, my family, my profession, and myself.

But what if I had lost or was alienated from my family, was being sued by the family of another patient who had committed suicide, was painfully aware of limitations imposed by aging, and felt truly seen and valued only during sessions with the patient with whom I was in love, who in turn felt understood and valued by me in a way she never had before? In this scenario I might try to convince myself that the love between me and my patient felt so right that it couldn't possibly be immoral. But I know enough about how colluding with a patient in mutual idealization works as a defensive resistance against potentially destabilizing unconscious hostility that I would have a hard time convincing myself it was OK. Moreover, the very fact that I had to put effort into convincing myself would alert me that I was trying to justify something that, however romantic and self-affirming it felt, also felt disturbingly wrong. This would in turn alert me to the fact that there must be a disturbing level of hostility threatening to emerge between my patient and me that we were seeking to avoid by converting the analytic relationship into a sexual courtship. And it would remind me of what I had been trying to convince myself to forget: that it is always morally wrong—the violation of a sacred trust—to have sex with a patient, just as it is always morally wrong to kill a patient or to have sex with a five-year-old child, no matter what the circumstances, no matter how powerful the emotions.

I come back then to where I started four paragraphs ago. Only if my brain were affected in such a way that I had absolutely no memory of what I now clearly understand and had lost the capacity to distinguish right from wrong, can I imagine ever having sex with a patient. But I can say this only because I do have the capacity to distinguish right from wrong. I know that I am capable of both love and tyranny and I can tell the difference between what is loving and what is tyrannical in my emotional impulses. I am confident that I can continue to recognize this difference even under the duress of powerful unconscious impulses. But I have this confidence only because I have done this kind of self-analysis in the heat of the therapeutic moment many times, and I am always to some degree on the alert for the intrusion of my own unconscious into the analytic process. Evenly hovering attention, as I understand and practice it, entails a constant level of relaxed but vigilant self-awareness. So the kind of self-scanning that Stanley Coen recommends, under the compassionately restraining guidance of my self-reflective moral consciousness, is central to the way I have always worked with patients.

My concern is that because it is missing in psychoanalytic theory, this higher consciousness may easily be missing in the inner life of a psychoanalyst, even a well-trained highly experienced psychoanalyst, without anyone being able to tell until there is an ethics violation to deal with. I think it is likely that many analysts never use their higher moral consciousness to do the necessary self-scanning. Some may not know how to do it because they are incapable of empathy and their only way of relating to people is to use them to serve their own narcissistic needs, which might include the need to think of themselves as caring, competent therapists even while having sex with their patients. This degree of narcissism no doubt does exist among analysts but I would like to believe that it is rare.

What seems more likely is that analysts would dismiss the need for self-scanning because they believe they are already well-enough analyzed to have rational control of their emotions; or that they would never recognize or use their higher consciousness because they deny the existence of a higher consciousness, or of an innate and universal moral sense. These analysts would deny that all human beings have an instinctive understanding of the Golden Rule, for example, or of Shakespeare's moral distinction between love and tyranny and Buber's very similar distinction between I-Thou mutual unfolding of selves versus I-It imposing of one self on another. Certainly this was true of Freud himself, who, in *Civilization and Its Discontents* "reject(s) the existence of an original, . . . natural, capacity to distinguish good from bad" (1930, p. 124). Freud believed that rationality but not morality is intrinsic to human nature, so it is not surprising that he could offer Dora only I-It objectifying theory-based explanations of her pathology but no I-Thou appreciation or respect for her dignity and wholeness as a person.

What then of analysts who are temperamentally or characterologically similar to Freud—who may be drawn to psychoanalysis precisely for the abstracting, distancing objectivity of its I-It theory, and who have little experience or appreciation of I-Thou mutuality in their lives? These analysts might not believe in morality or free will because like Freud, they believe that all motivation is ultimately reducible to drive-gratification, limited only by societally imposed constraints that are internalized out of fear. Or they might believe that ethical codes are no more than arbitrary social constructions. So they wouldn't think of a sexual boundary violation as a violation of a sacred trust because they wouldn't hold anything sacred. Or they might believe that no clear distinction can be made between right and wrong, good and evil, because every motivated act is a compromise formation that integrates conflicting elements of libido and aggression. Any of these attitudes and beliefs would make a psychoanalyst more vulnerable to committing sexual boundary violations, not because he wouldn't recognize it when he became sexually aroused, but because he wouldn't recognize it as immoral to act on his arousal.

I realize that many of the analysts who have sexual relations with their patients feel consciously what they believe is love for the patient. Similarly, many of the Catholic priests and many of the parents who have sexual relations with the children in their care feel consciously what they believe is love for the child. The problem is that none of these perpetrators is sufficiently alarmed by the fact that their feeling of love is accompanied by sexual arousal. Their socially constructed, fear-based superego too easily allows them to use their feeling of love to rationalize their arousal and then to rationalize the tyrannical misuse of power to which their arousal impels them. Without an inner moral compass to guide them, they cannot recognize or distinguish between the conflicting impulses of love and tyranny embodied in their sexual desire. They have no deeply felt conviction that it is always wrong, always destructive, to use another person for their own sexual or narcissistic needs, disregarding that person's needs, especially so when that person is a patient who has entrusted him or herself to their care.

HOW SHALL WE FIND THE CONCORD OF THIS DISCORD?

If we want all psychoanalysts to understand that sexual boundary violations are not only prohibited by our code of ethics but always morally wrong, then psychoanalysis needs a better theory: one which views not only sexual desire but moral consciousness as intrinsic to human nature; a theory that acknowledges and explains how human beings develop the capacity not only for neurotic fear-based guilt but also for authentic guilt, based on genuine remorse for misusing a fellow human being who is as much deserving of love and respect as we are. The elements of such a theory can be found in our literature. For example, the accepting non-judgmental attitude of Coen's superego that informs his method of self-scanning is an intrinsically moral stance, entailing a systematic application of the Golden Rule. Historically, psychoanalysis has considered this accepting non-judgmental attitude the ideal stance of the analyst toward the patient, but we have had to disguise and hide from ourselves its intrinsic morality by calling it 'technical neutrality.' Nevertheless, the expectation that an analyst will be non-judgmental and remain 'equidistant' from the patient's id, ego, and superego is in essence nothing less than a moral imperative: to treat our patients with an attitude of acceptance, respect, and compassion for every aspect of who they are. What 'equal distance from id, ego, and superego' really requires is equal empathy and respect for the id and superego sides of whatever conflict the patient is experiencing *and* for the compromise formation (the ego adaptation) that the patient is needing to use in order to manage the conflict.

This equi-empathic attitude was notable by its absence in Freud's treatment of Dora. It requires of the analyst an accepting, non-imposing

'I-Thou' awareness that at the 'dynamic center' of the patient is an energy
of unfolding and actualization that has its own direction and moral compass, expressing itself even in his apparent pathology. It entails trusting—in fact knowing—that we don't need to intervene to prevent the
patient's superego or his id from causing harm, or to 'guide' his ego in a
more adaptive direction, because the *right* direction is inherent in his
unfolding personhood, in the innate 'maturational process' of his 'true
self' (Summers, 2001; Hoffman, 2004). Even the problem that is currently
interrupting the patient's maturation—the symptoms or dysfunction
created by his unconscious conflict—is at the same time an expression of
this maturational striving toward actualization. His conflicting unconscious emotions embody powerful motivational energy that is unsafe to
use as long as the emotions remain unconscious, because it may produce
impulsive or unreflective immoral action—hence the need for a debilitat-
ing symptom or inhibition. As the emotions become conscious, however,
the patient can use their energy self-reflectively, to resolve his conflict
with moral integrity and thus further his unfolding and actualization.
However regressed or symptomatic the patient may be, therefore, we
need only to facilitate his process of self-unfolding, using Coen's method
of self-scanning so that, first, we and then the patient can safely feel the
disturbing, conflict-engendering emotions and can tap into the maturational energy they embody. In doing so, we trust that the patient can and
will discover from within not only what is right for him but what is
morally right as well.

Melanie Klein's theory that the depressive position unfolds naturally
out of the paranoid-schizoid position implies the same kind of trust that
human beings have an innate direction not only of sexual but of moral
development; a direction that includes the innate moral tendency to feel
remorse (authentic guilt) for wanting to harm someone we love. Howard
Covitz's proposed revision of Freud's oedipal theory (Covitz, 1998, Frattaroli, 2008) elaborates on this proto-morality of Klein's depressive position. Covitz views the oedipal conflict as in effect the birth of moral
consciousness in the child's awareness of his conflicting impulses of tyranny and love. The standard understanding of the oedipus complex is
deficient, says Covitz, in viewing the oedipal child as narcissistically focused on need-gratification, forced to renounce that gratification only out
of fear but without ever having to renounce the fundamental narcissistic
attitude that his own need is the only one that matters. On the contrary,
argues Covitz, the developmental shift required of the oedipal child is
not from drive-gratification to socialized renunciation but from narcissism to empathy and mutuality, with the child's narcissistic (tyrannical)
need to impose his will on both parents giving way to a more loving and
empathic appreciation of his parents as separate individuals who have
their own needs and their own independent relationship.

I have argued elsewhere (1990, 2001) that, notwithstanding Freud's official rejection of the idea, the existence of an innate moral sense is an implicit and essential element in Freudian theory. As a matter of simple logic, an innate moral sense is a necessary condition for the development of an internalized Freudian superego. The internalization of moral precepts from family and society could not occur without a pre-existing moral sense to serve as a kind of template for moral concepts. Otherwise, humans would have no need for and could never have developed words like 'right and wrong,' 'good and evil'—as opposed to 'permitted and forbidden'—because we would have no capacity to recognize the moral categories to which these words refer. This logic is analogous to that of the argument that humans would not be capable of destructive aggression, even in reaction to traumatizing experiences, unless there were some kind of 'instinct' or neurobiological program for revenge/retaliation (which is the root motive and 'justification' for all destructive aggression) already present in human nature waiting to be activated by painful, revenge-provoking experiences.

I have proposed, in addition (2001), that just as the seeds of Waelder's and Coen's "higher consciousness" superego were present but unintegrated in Freud's "On Narcissism," so too the seeds of a psychoanalytic theory of morality were present but unintegrated in Freud's so-called dual instinct theory of Eros and the death instinct (Freud, 1920). Freud often described Eros as an extension of libido, a more generalized way to describe the tension-discharging, homeostasis-maintaining motivation of the sexual drive. As he actually defined it, however, Eros represented a radically new kind of motivation—an organismic need for energy-increasing integration and a more personal need for connection and community—that was diametrically opposed to the idea of an impersonal libido needing to be discharged according to the constancy/pleasure principle. Nevertheless, Freud insisted that it was the death instinct, not Eros, that constituted a new motivation 'beyond the pleasure principle.' The problem is that Freud was conflicted about the radical change he was trying to make in his theory and his conflict created a profound confusion in him (and in psychoanalysis to this day) about the true meaning of Eros and of the death instinct.

Not only did Freud define Eros as the direct opposite of a tension-reducing drive toward low-energy constancy or homeostasis. He defined the death instinct as an exact facsimile of such a drive, based on what he now called the 'Nirvana principle,' a tendency of the organism to reduce energy to the lowest possible steady state (ultimately death). In other words the death instinct was a principle of tension-discharge and homeostasis, an undisguised restatement of Freud's original constancy/pleasure principle! In fact Freud recognized and acknowledged that the Nirvana principle and the constancy/pleasure principle were identical, yet he was unable or unwilling to draw the obvious conclusion.

What Freud *should* have concluded is that the sexual drive (and human motivation generally) includes two distinct conflicting elements—the I-Thou element of love and the I-It element of lust, the desire to come together in intimate communion and the self-centered need to use or be used for purposes of tension-relieving discharge. Sabina Spielrein had already given Freud this idea in 1912, when she proposed that the sexual drive includes conflicting instincts of transformation and destruction. Freud could then have expanded the concept of tension-relieving lust to include blood lust (revenge) and the lust for power (tyranny) as well as sexual lust. Had he done so, the concept of a death instinct would have made a good deal more sense. It would have helped explain why inner conflicts over sexuality are universal, for instance—because sexual desire always contains elements of both love and lust—and shed new light on the biblical link between sexual desire and the knowledge of good and evil. The problem was that, in so doing, it would also have shifted the meaning of Eros and the death instinct from that of value-free, ostensibly scientific, motivational principles to that of moral categories. The very distinction between love and lust, after all, is primarily a moral distinction—between I-Thou mutuality and I-It using/imposing on (with the important qualification that I-It lustful using is not immoral if it is a mutual I-It element within an I-Thou relationship). So it would have been difficult for Freud to draw the parallel between Eros/Thanatos and love/lust without moving psychoanalysis openly into the realm of moral philosophy. He would have had to admit the amoral hedonism of his old libido concept and highlight the spiritual significance of Eros: as a force in human nature working not only toward love, community, and healing but toward a higher moral consciousness as well.

I am suggesting that the true direction of Freud's theorizing, implicit in his dual-instinct theory properly understood, was toward including in his account of human nature an innate program of moral development to complement the more familiar instinctual program of psychosexual development. Freud's conflict theory would then be best understood as a universal moral conflict between love and lust (Shakespeare's love versus tyranny, Buber's mutual unfolding versus imposition). This reformulation is entirely consistent with Freud's theory of the *origin* of inner conflict and the birth of civilization as he proposed it in *Civilization and Its Discontents* (1930). Borrowing from Darwin, Freud argued that prior to the development of civilization, prehistoric man must have lived as many animals do, in social groups controlled through power and fear by a tyrannically dominating 'alpha male'—the primal father. There would have been no inner conflict in such a pre-human 'primal horde' because humanoids had not yet developed beyond animal consciousness. There would have been no sense of morality, no cultural values, no social taboos, and no superego to internalize these values and taboos. Freud then speculated that at some point a group of primal sons must have risen up in rebellion to kill the alpha-male primal father, driven both by lust for the women he controlled and by envy of his power to control them. At that moment, Freud imagined, individual conscience and cultural taboo (i.e., the superego) must have come into being simultaneously. How? Through the great *remorse* the brothers would have felt immediately after their murderous deed. Now presumably, such primal murders could have occurred many times previously without provoking any remorse— as they do among lions, for instance—but conscience, inner conflict, and civilization could not have begun until human nature had evolved to the point that it was capable of remorse.

In this theory the first fully human experience of inner conflict did not involve an internalized superego producing neurotic guilt. It involved an internally generated feeling of remorse—authentic guilt—that came *before* the establishment of any internalizable values or taboos. So it could not have been produced by Freud's internalized superego-conscience but was produced rather by the birth of Waelder's and Coen's superego-higher consciousness. This higher consciousness expressed itself both in the innate, unconditioned love the sons felt for their father, and in the feeling of remorse that signaled their new awareness of the moral incompatibility between this innate love and the instinctive tyrannical lust that had driven them to murder their father. In that sense, Freud's myth of the primal murder is a more viscerally compelling version of biblical myth of 'the Fall.' Just as Adam and Eve acquire the knowledge of good and evil (the hallmark of Coen's higher consciousness) through the shame they feel after their willfully defiant act of narcissistic self-assertion, Freud's primal sons acquire it through the remorse they feel over their murderously defiant act of self-assertion, and the awareness it brings of their conflicting purposes of love and lust.

Psychoanalysis understands these myths of what once happened in our distant past as metaphorical ways of accounting for what is continually happening at the deepest level of our present being. At this level we all have conflicting motives of love and lust, and we all have a higher consciousness that can discern the moral difference between them. So the alarming frequency with which senior analysts commit egregious sexual boundary violations shows that human beings can be unconscious not only of what is lowest in us but also of what is highest. Stanley Coen has explained and illustrated how psychoanalysts can use our higher-consciousness superego to prevent such immoral violations in our practice. But clearly there are many psychoanalysts who do not understand or have conscious access to a higher-consciousness superego or who do not feel it necessary to do the kind of superego-informed self-scanning that Coen recommends, or even to maintain a proper psychoanalytic attitude of non-judgmental 'neutrality.'

This widespread failure of moral consciousness and good faith practice among psychoanalysts would not be possible, I believe, if moral consciousness and moral development were essential and *explicit* elements in our theory and standards of practice. As it is, the amorality of our theory makes it far too easy for psychoanalysts to rationalize and justify sexual boundary violations to themselves. It encourages them to conceptualize therapy only as an I-It application of a theory-based technique and *not* also as an I-Thou process of helping patients to unfold what is already nascent within them. Without this I-Thou attitude and awareness to humanize our work, an exclusively I-It psychoanalytic stance can too easily allow us to impose a narcissistically invested theory on patients we treat like cases—as Freud did to Dora—or worse, to impose our narcissistically invested sexuality on patients who become the objects of our desire.

PSYCHOANALYSIS NEEDS A SEA CHANGE

If we are to be serious about preventing sexual boundary violations, I would argue that we have to change the psychoanalytic culture and the psychoanalytic philosophy that currently make such transgressions so easy to commit and rationalize. We have to acknowledge and agree upon the core psychoanalytic values embodied in Coen's superego and in his method of self-scanning. This would include acknowledging that the capacity for genuinely loving mutuality—*not* a preference for genital sexuality—indicates a successful resolution of the Oedipus complex; and that 'technical neutrality' has always been a covert expression of our core values of compassion, respect, and moral discernment. Moreover, we would have to acknowledge that these psychoanalytic values are not only professional guidelines that further the treatment, but moral values that further the treatment *because* they are the necessary condition for any healing relationship and more generally because they define the right way for human beings to treat each other.

We have to make it officially unacceptable for a psychoanalyst to graduate an accredited training institute without demonstrating that he or she understands and practices these core psychoanalytic values. Crucial elements in such a change would be first, to explicitly incorporate Coen's and Waelder's higher-consciousness superego into our theory—which would entail adding to our theory the concept of an innate moral sense and an innate line of moral development; and second, to incorporate Coen's method of superego-informed self-scanning as our most important standard of psychoanalytic practice, expecting it to be taught in every supervision and demonstrated in every full psychoanalytic case report.

EIGHT

Guilt and Its Vicissitudes: A Concluding Commentary

Jeanne Bailey, Ph.D.

The contributions on the experience of guilt by William Singletary, Desy Safán-Gerard, and Stanley Coen accentuate the acceptance of our vulnerabilities and tolerance of our destructive feelings toward others. This allows us to bring such dystonic phenomena into consciousness in order to work with them. They highlight recognizing feelings of helplessness and anxiety as protection against enactment as well as providing more access to deeper layers of the mind through an ability to bear guilt beside a good conscience which guides us through painful realities in our work.

Singletary takes up two kinds of conscience. A good conscience helps us make growth-promoting choices which accept painful realities while feeling sadness and remorseful guilt. He suggests this comes out of an environment of loving connections and safety. A bad conscience comes out of an environment of hatred, omnipotence, and control which denies need and sadness. As per Wurmser (1994, 2007), change comes from suffering through massive inner conflict of conscience through insight, action, and work on behalf of somebody else or a great cause. The recognition of destructive damaging attacks allows us to cherish rather than trash, accept shortcomings, and forgive as in good guilt.

He describes work with two boys who come to recognize the need for a first aid kit when we hurt, even in our hearts, people we love. We can then turn loving into hating and back into loving feelings. He notes that hurting those we love and need most is a defense against feeling sad and needy and leads to punitive self-destructiveness. In our work with patients, we take on the small, still voice who guides our patients toward acceptance of reality as we take up the defenses against affect and a loving attitude in the transference. The repetition of recognizing our hateful destructive treatment of others over and over again in the analytic work is described in his lengthy treatment of an isolated boy who resorts to violent fantasies before becoming a young man with a self-regulating system which accepts the ongoing presence of caring others and seeks connection with others. This treatment is paralleled with the story of Pinocchio, in which a wooden boy becomes a real-life boy resembling the entrapment in literature and psychoanalysis which requires salvaging.

Safán-Gerard tells us interpretation of defenses against guilt fails to help our patients tolerate guilt and leads to arrested development and regressive movement. She asserts a tendency to meet attacks from our patients with interpretive attacks which focus on aggressive destructiveness and risk sado-masochistic enactments. Loving concern is inherent in feelings of guilt and may be expressed in fleeting and subtle manners. She elaborates through clinical material how the analyst's acknowledgment of their own experiences through countertransference is essential to decreasing destructiveness and increasing loving feelings in our patients. While Klein (1933, 1937, 1940) and Freud (1914, 1915, 1923) point out aggressive impulses toward the object, Klein adds the initiation of reparative efforts toward external and internal objects when the aggressive impulses become conscious rather than Freud's idea of unconscious guilt which seeks punishment. Guilt becomes a necessary response to the awareness of destructiveness. Mere awareness of destructive impulses risks viewing the analyst as the external superego figure leading to masochistic submission.

Working with this countertransference allows the analyst to note their own defensive withdrawal from accepting positions involving helplessness at the hands of defeating others. When this helplessness is not worked with internally by the analyst and left out of awareness, the analyst risks these defensive counterattacks which increase the analysand's defensive retreat. By taking us through clinical material including her own acceptance and working through of her taken-aback reactivity, she highlights the importance of recognizing our own position relative to the material presented. She also describes the importance of working with envy and highlights a different view of guilt. Rather than seeking punishment as Freud proposed, guilt represents a shift toward concern for the other which provides entry into reparative care and relatedness with others while accepting need and helplessness.

Coen similarly addresses the need to look inward for our own vulnerabilities with an optimal superego stance in order to attend to our patient's unconscious. He suggests our ability to identify with rather than distance from the vulnerabilities in our patients as well as our colleagues prepares us for managing our own vulnerabilities and guards against potential transgressions to meet narcissistic needs. He suggests our analyses may not be sufficient and we must be open to reverie and feelings of anxiety, helplessness, and hatred in order to continue to work them through. He gives examples of awareness and trial identifications which allow us to manage our narcissistic needs by accessing superego signals which deepens our work with patients.

Fear of managing the heat if we let ourselves regress beside our analysands and taste their struggles may close off the progress in an analysis. He suggests seamless clinical presentations create a myth of magical understanding. When we are unaware of our struggles or seek to deny the possibility of similar needs and impulses, we close off this deeper understanding and risk boundary violations.

TWO KINDS OF CONSCIENCE

Singletary tells us about a good conscience directing us toward choices which accept painful realities and open the door to sad and remorseful guilt. He contrasts this with a bad conscience, which denigrates work and dependency, fears attack, and leads to self-punishment. He elaborates omnipotence and hostility as defenses against dependency and need. "I would stress the inclination to attack, tear down, or destroy those we love and need as an attempt to control loss, vulnerability, and sadness."

He tells us how stories and mythology are psychological developmental guides to manage universal issues around feeling states and internal crises. In his work with children, their play illuminates needing "a first aid kit in your heart for when we hurt, even in our hearts, people we love." Another boy who has difficulty giving and receiving love calls him the love doctor who works with him on "how loving feelings get changed into hating feelings and how hating feelings get changed back into loving feelings." He suggests the courage to face fears and risk loving and being loved promotes ego-strength and self-regulation by building up "feelings muscles." Tolerating sadness rather than hatred is important in object constancy per Mahler, Pine, and Bergman (1975), when one chooses to love in the face of painful affects.

A talented boy diagnosed with Asperger's evolves, through their fifteen years of work together, from a child who rejects and destroys loving help into a talented song-writer, who is transformed like Pinocchio from a wooden boy to a young man who looks for love he can use with "your voice inside my head . . . because now I'm winning (since) I have something to lose." This boy entered treatment in a frightened, overly dependent, and isolated state that involved retreats into fantasies of violence and conflict. The burden of his emotional state was conveyed through a drawing of the Titanic hitting the iceberg and a worry about the table holding up under all the toys he put there. He noted his early non-caring selfish stance "like a knot you can't unwind" which the analyst understood as rooted in his fears of uncertainty. The story of Pinocchio resonated with him and was read repeatedly during their treatment.

Singletary describes Pinocchio's journey from a "wooden, out-of-control, uncaring and self-centered puppet [who] becomes able to give and receive love." His journey is compared to psychoanalytic therapy, described by Shengold (2004) as developing the non-sexual caring about self and others. Pinocchio discards or destroys offerings of love from Geppetto who sacrificed to provide for him. Instead, Pinocchio follows the destructive figures of the Fox and Cat.

Interpreting conflicts surrounding love within the transference opens new developmental experiences both within and outside the treatment setting. Comparing computer default operating systems to those for self-regulation, Singletary suggests early experiences dominated by safety and loving connections become self-systems of loving, humility, and acceptance of vulnerability. In contrast, experiences based on hatred, omnipotence, power, and control lead to self-systems which deny need and sadness beside a destructively punitive and lenient conscience. He posits the central process between patient and analysis is the repeated giving and receiving of love or empathic concern to facilitate tolerance of loving and being loved.

Representations of imprisoned figures as in Dante's lower rungs of hell who are frozen and unable to move are compared to Pinocchio and our own analysands who are often described as imprisoned and in need of rescue from trapped positions through salvage operations per Meltzer (1968). He also refers to Rosenfeld's (1971) description of rescuing sane dependent part of self trapped in psychotic narcissistic structures.

Pinocchio's entrapment is due to the trauma of loss, threat, and deprivation. There is no mother, and poverty and death continually threaten him. In the story, Pinocchio repeatedly turns away from loving connections to follow seductive, untrustworthy, and ultimately destructive figures. Eventually, he recognizes his part in damaging helpful figures, experiences sadness, and begins to repair the damage through work and care of Geppetto. Singletary refers to the sadness at the grave of the good fairy and Jiminy Cricket with the 'small still voice' which is not too harsh and helps us recognize and accept painful realities about ourselves and feel a sad, remorseful guilt for out destructiveness.

In the first six months, his young patient expresses hope to be normal like the analyst and his father. The analyst notes the helpful presence of the parents and himself as well as the boy's own efforts. He tells us this after mentioning the ongoing retreats to isolated fantasy and jumping as well as resisting the analyst's attempts to understand him. The analyst understands his uncooperativeness as a fear of needing and depending while turning instead to disparaging their work. When the boy discounts requested water by pointing out "you didn't give me food!" the analyst calls his response a 'thank you.' Singletary tells us meeting the request interfered with the boy's sense of omnipotence and interfered with true gratitude. He emphasizes the importance of interpreting the ego-weakening protections which involve attacks on the helper due to envy and greed.

A birthday party for a favorite puppet is followed by various attacks on the puppet which is then eaten. The analyst comments: The puppet you love so much is now inside. He tells us of the need to be sad and miss them rather than just mad. Another story involves a policeman who helps his enemy. The enemy shoots the policeman and the patient describes shame in the enemy character for the first time. The policeman becomes a psychologist and warden at a prison which helps people through loving and caring to be free.

As he turns sixteen, the patient begins writing songs which describe how he has felt shackled to the self-destructive burying of his feelings. He can only take a shot at uncovering them which he recognizes is insufficient. In another song, he notes his retreat from painful realities which means "[watching] life drive by [rather than] breathe like the rest," which moves him toward ongoing connection in seeing "my arms around you though there's no one there." He now recognizes the "sweet lie of ignorant bliss."

Singletary highlights the difficulties of the work and notes consolidated work at school followed by withdrawal when the structure of school was gone. The patient describes "trying to take something that tears you apart, then create something out of it, then sometimes it's hard to keep self together." We hear the "small still voice" of the analyst who points out choices made in non-critical and inviting ways. We also hear his pleasure in the creativity of his patient. "I took it all in, but I told myself I don't wanna lose it this time . . . is this the art of losing or just the price of living . . . waste not the lessons learned cause you're still alive and you're only stronger."

SADO-MASOCHISTIC ENACTMENTS

In her contribution, Dr. Safán-Gerard elaborates guilt as evidence of the growing capacity for concern for the other. The fear of managing accompanied feeling-states triggers old patterns of defensive withdrawal. She highlights recognizing fleeting concerns as an essential step to the progression of relating to others through tolerating the guilt. Mere focus on the defenses against guilt risks entrance into a sado-masochistic enactment.

The patient expiates the guilt and (fails to recognize) what he or she does to his or her objects. The analyst's concern with the patient's defenses against the emergence of conscious guilt needs to be balanced by an equal attention to the patient's incipient experience of guilt and the loving feelings embodied in this guilt.

The ability to tolerate guilt and allow entrance into consciousness occurs through the diminishment of destructiveness and mobilization of love. By listening for this concern for the other the analyst helps develop the care for the complexes of the other. This working-through of the wish to differentiate occurs by understanding the tendency to resort to the familial manner of managing feelings through catharsis and denial in order to support an old need to remain connected to his important object. She posits awareness of concern as a mitigator of aggression and destructiveness which invites integration rather than withdrawal and turning upon one's self. This elaboration of technique invites consideration of the struggle to maintain contact with the important object while experiencing that object as separate with their own concerns and struggles which comes out of a growing ability to accept one's own concerns through the analytic work with another.

Safán-Gerard points out that love and hate are coming together and 'love begins to surmount hate.' She reminds us of

> Freud's notion of unconscious guilt as a search for punishment. [For Klein] guilt becomes the driving force of depressive anxiety [from prior hostile attacks on the loved object] . . . manifest[ing] . . . as conscious guilt . . . a "marker of development . . . that typically initiates reparative action toward the external [and] internal object." . . . "if projected onto the analyst . . . the patient becomes a victim of the sadism perceived in the analyst."

If we consider guilt as the outcome of an unrealistically harsh superego as in Freud's model, the analyst works to free the analysand from this demanding and harsh internal voice. In Klein's model, the goal is to facilitate bearing the guilt in order to begin reparation. In Safán-Gerard's view, mere facilitation of awareness of guilt risks colluding with this harsh superego and trapping the patient into masochistic submission. Limiting awareness to aggressive attacks which seek punishment bypasses the opportunity to explore the 'besiegement' of concern for the other as well as abandoned parts of oneself. The analyst resorts to punishing and condemning interpretations in response to the projected sadistic impulses. Impasses occur when the analyst's frustrations lead to self-condemnation against their own feelings of hatred leading to guilt and even masochistic surrender to the patient.

Managing these projections of destructiveness requires concern for the analysand as well as acceptance of the analyst's own guilt. Without these concerns, the use of interpretation becomes a sadistic tool to give the destructiveness back to the analysand. Through Steiner (1990) and Riesenberg (1981), she reminds us that linking our own states of anxiety and confusion to guilt for attacks on our previous objects and our wish to repair them helps us manage projective identifications. The analyst may need to point out the guilt as evidence of love without losing sight of the underlying destructiveness. One must have empathy for the love and the hatred expressed which comes out of accepting one's own hatred and love for the patient and our own previous objects.

Safán-Gerard further links awareness of love as bringing to bear the dependency upon and separateness from the absent mother which threatens a sense of autonomy. Analysts may use interpretations to distance and retain their own sense of autonomy. In parallel, a patient's rejection of an interpretation is an attempt to avoid infantile dependency along with the painful experience of rejection or amplified rejections by parents with unmodulated aggression. The patient resorts to old patterns of managing their destructiveness through denial and inflating or deflating the self as a superior or worthless individual who does not need or even deserve the absence of regard. The "reluctance to admit to loving [is an attempt to avoid] the resultant anxiety of depending on an object, and the fear of losing a hard-won autonomy."

Her patient uses intellectual defenses to involve the analyst as a mere observer of his analytic sophistication while evading emotional awareness. Excitement for him leads him to a wish for triumph over others and spoils their good feelings for him. Any desire to be part of a couple is projected and envy prevents experiencing gratitude for the help and understanding he receives. He avoids awareness of his use of the others to avoid experiencing guilt and exclude awareness of his need.

He owes the analyst money. The analyst realizes interruption of the treatment would collude with his attempt to see the analyst as uncaring and let him off the hook from realizing his own usage. He revokes a moment of guilty awareness of using his girlfriend. He shifts to the various ways he does without while others take advantage including the analyst who he imagines seeks to rob him. The analyst feels derailed by his shift and fails to interpret the difficulty, staying with his experience of love for his girlfriend which creates guilt over his use of her. He shifts to his reluctance to enter into involvements which 'don't pan out' and his superiority of only caring for himself. The analyst feels irritated and wants to shake him out of his aristocratic stance. Pointing out how he lives off his girlfriend and seeks pity from the analyst, she falls into chastising him for his psychopathy and colludes with his presentation of himself as uncaring and callous. His subsequent offer to pay up, while suggesting analysis is a form of his aristocratic stance, is seen as a denial of guilt and not wanting to bear witness to his use of others and as avoiding recognizing the underlying love involved. The analyst interprets his expatiation of guilt through the deserved punishment of low resources whereby guilt is expiated without suffering. His dependent self is projected through his acknowledgment of helping suffering others which avoids his own dependency as well as his jealousy and envy for what is provided.

She notes her interpretation could have centered on his fear of being the dependent baby who cannot control his objects and resorts to an aristocratic self who imagines he needs no one. Interpretation of a dream represents his greedy and reckless self who is also sad over the effect on the father. An affair is interpreted as his inability to control his girlfriend and get what he needs from her. This invites recognition of his struggle between omnipotence and more mature solutions that accept the need of and caring for the other. She further elaborates her identification with the women in his life as like her own damaged and rejected mother with the analysand as the rejecting father. She recognizes how her unconscious hatred led to masochistic surrender to his neglect as evidenced by the accumulation of debt which serves to offset her own guilt through punishment. She goes on to say that rather than focusing on the defenses against guilt the emphasis should be on the incipient experience of guilt however fleeting it may be, which would meet up with Klein's idea of maximum anxiety. Asking for and listening to the details of the guilt helps the patient to bear it. While containing does not alter the guilt, our invitation may illuminate how the patient tries to cure himself and allow for further interpretation of underlying conflicts. According to Safán-Gerard, these interpretations of the management of guilt provide an anchor which prevents or delays a shift backward and facilitates staying in the depressive position. Hence, guilt is a useful primary focus of interpretation when it encompasses anxiety, guilt, and reparation. Acknowledging attacks due to envy or jealousy allows the guilt to become conscious and bearable while idealization of destructiveness and ruthlessness increases unconscious guilt.

Hatred due to envy and jealousy creates a wish to spoil and devalue as a means of managing narcissistic injury. Actual experience of the jealousy and envy is more effective in preventing their use in unconscious destructiveness and prevents attack on the devalued and spoiled internal objects who can then stop representing 'not having what it takes.' Once this diminishes, an analysand may be able to experience guilt including loving concern for these objects and allow reparation.

THE ANALYST'S SUPEREGO

Dr. Coen highlights the value of acknowledging our own needs, wishes, and temptations to facilitate access of our analysand's unconscious minds. Restraint comes to bear through our love for our patients as we let in these experiences. He suggests the danger of accepting our own analyses as an adequate vehicle for sufficient modification of our needs with no danger of acting upon them. Also, distancing from analysts who fall prey to their vulnerabilities through even non-sexual boundary violations suggests our inability to identify with the propensity in us for a similar fate. In fact, a distrust of our ability to monitor ourselves sufficiently may cause us to distance from accessing our unconscious through open listening and risk such an enactment. He suggests trial identifications with analysts who have succumbed may help us identify and practice how we would manage our vulnerabilities in such situations. We are all at risk for such violations when we are sufficiently needy and vulnerable as per Gabbard and Lester (1995). In addition, tolerance of our own needs, wishes, and temptations invites deeper inquiry with our patients.

Developing our confidence to contain our own needs and desires requires experiencing deep longings and learning they can be subsumed within our mature responsible selves. Then, we can recognize them as temptations without ominous action. Experiencing the anxiety around temptations allows us to say no to them.

He describes characteristic trouble arising from analysts who were indulged as children without protective limits followed by analyses which did not deal with these absent limits and repetitive entitled wishes. Superego signals like anxiety, guilt, self-criticism, shame, and imitation must be met with restraint and concern for the patient's needs above our own. Obsessive torment may signal a risk for transgression. A tolerant, loving attitude enables the analyst to help his patient tolerate and then modify and resolve conflict.

Candidates, in particular, may have difficulty bearing their analysands' neediness and hatred as they are themselves new to managing these feelings. In an example, two pregnant candidate analysts learn to bear their patients' hateful wishes after women analysts shared their experiences at a discussion group at the American Psychoanalytic Association. This facilitation is contrasted with the intolerance imposed by public presentations of seemingly effortless analytic work. This conveys a myth which may encourage analysts to push away from their own disturbances. While seeking consultation reduces the risk of misusing patients, the analyst must be able to recognize a problem of extricating or perpetuating inevitable enactments.

If we imagine ourselves into the clinical scene of others' work and grasp our own potential vulnerability, we accept such difficulty with more readiness and equanimity. Coen encourages talking openly with our patients in order to normalize anxiety and distress. In addition, Celenza (2007) advocates attending to shifts in power and mutuality. In contrast, our distance and dissociation suggest continued vigilance threatens us. He reminds us of McLaughlin's (2005) work to manage pushing away from the homoerotic cravings of an analysand. He realized the deep impact of his early loss of his father and his own unaddressed cravings which went unrecognized in two analyses.

Freud (1912) advised that the analyst should simply listen and not bother about whether he is keeping anything in mind. The analyst:

> should withhold all conscious influences from his capacity to attend and give himself over completely to his unconscious memory . . . [in order to be] a receptive organ towards the transmitting unconscious of the patient.

Coen describes poets and Shakespearian scholars who highlight listening to sounds and getting carried away by 'giddy oscillations.' Faimberg (1996) listens to how her patients listen to her. Chodorow (2003) differentiates 'listening for' from "listening to."

While Freud (1912) encouraged free listening, he reminded us that we must also be aware of our complexes which interfere and recognize that our control "is not so complete that we may not suddenly one day go further than we had intended." The analyst needs access to his own unconscious while recognizing the possibility of being carried away. Perhaps this worry of being carried away holds us back in being 'unconditionally open to ourselves' per Parsons. How much murderous hatred, sexual arousal, detachment, and shared narcissistic specialness, talent or celebrity can we manage?

Coen posits that denial and minimization limit our ability to experience the anxiety and mistrust that would help us manage our impulses. Our narcissistic needs may even include our use of theory. He cites Kite's (2008) reminder that much of our character is out of our conscious awareness and therefore impossible to manage. But the analyst can scan the edges through attending to feelings, sensations, concerns, images, fantasies, language, songs, daydreams, night-dreams. Searles (1986) encouraged 'a no-holds-barred' approach. Yet, too much scrutiny can also be problematic in taking the focus away from the patient and onto the analyst. However, the temptation to say 'not me' according to Sullivan (1953) and Stern (2010) may lead us away from understanding something in our analysands and even risk enactment.

Coen tells us our love for analysis must also accept the hatred, disappointment, and pain in order to remain responsible for what we wish to eliminate in ourselves. Through Stern, he reminds us: what we cannot bear in ourselves, we cannot see in our patients. Enactments both express and hide what analysts cannot face. In an example, his awareness of feeling blown off by a supervisee introduced the parallel process of the supervisee feeling blown off by her patient. Accepting a reverie about Leo Stone (1961) while listening to a clinical presentation allowed recognition of the current distance in an otherwise warm analyst. Recognizing his own anxiety, helplessness, and rage after a patient's critical treatment of him allowed him to feel a desire to rid himself of this patient as well as go after him aggressively in a caring manner. This allowed understanding of his patient's longing for a father who could show his care through loud and aggressive proclamations and the ability to note defenses against affects.

In a previous paper on narcissistic temptations, colleagues argued against Coen's critical tone, proclaiming the need for room to cross boundaries 'consciously and deliberately' without excessive torment. Recognizing the dangers of too little and too much superego-ishness, he emphasizes tracking what lies outside of conscious awareness through an adaptive and flexible interaction with his superego in order to utilize signals without paralysis or constriction. Tolerating affects helps us understand what the patient needs. Denial of our wish to regress with the patient can lead to transgressions. Instead we need to tackle the impossible child in all of us.

CONCLUDING REMARKS

Singletary, Safán-Gerard, and Coen emphasize loving attitudes in order to bring hating, destructive attitudes into consciousness to forge stronger connections to ourselves and others. These authors elaborate the clinical processes involved to internalize Sterba's (1934) softer superego, loosen Loewald (1960) and Fraiberg's (1982) ego-weakening denial of painful realities which prevent internalization, or resolve Ornstein's (1974) dread to repeat. These clinical papers describe how we might join our patients in defending against needs and vulnerabilities based upon our ability to self-observe in an accepting manner.

Singletary describes two different consciences which depend on the developmental matrix of loving concern versus hating, controlling omnipotence. Coen suggests we need an optimal superego stance within ourselves in order to work with the fringes of our conscious minds and reach the depths of our patients' minds. Acceptance, guidance, love, praise, and restraint are essential to this analytic stance. For Safán-Gerard, guilt is evidence of loving attitudes which can bridge destructive tendencies toward our objects allowing for reparations and relatedness to others.

Suggesting analysts can enter into sado-masochistic enactments, Safán-Gerard thinks vulnerable objects from our past get stirred up by our patients' disparaging attitudes. Bringing our vulnerability from past objects into our awareness prevents us from acting destructively toward injuring objects. Recognizing her dreaded state of helplessness allowed her to listen for the glimmers of guilt for harms done by her patient. She could understand her trigger through identification with her mother and tolerate her own harm of her patient through interpretation of his destructiveness. She could then begin reparation rather than repeating the sado-masochistic cycle.

For Safán-Gerard, we manage our own hatred through accessible guilt which involves care for our patients. Then, we can accept our own feelings of helplessness with sadness and humility rather than strident admonitions. Singletary's statement of "needing to recognize one's shortcomings, feeling a good sense of guilt, the experience of forgiveness, and of developing a good heart" parallels Coen's emphasis of the supportive presence which affirms the difficulty of tolerating patient's needy, hateful wishes to invade and destroy and stretches the superego to become a helpful guide toward tolerating 'what is most difficult for the analyst to bear.'

Safán-Gerard agrees with Coen that interpretations may serve other purposes and get us away from the noisy sounds of despair into misguided abstractions. Coen highlights the value of hearing colleagues describe their struggle, which Safán-Gerard gives us a very good example of. We can infer Singletary's struggle to remain the small, still voice of Jiminy Cricket. We can appreciate the complexity of working with these attacks without becoming overbearing, distant, critical, or impatient through his interpretations which give a nudge toward accepting the need of others with gratitude.

Singletary tolerates rejection and disparaging treatment of his attempts to understand. He describes the price his patient pays for his idiosyncratic jumping up and down. He emphasizes hope through guiding relationships and his patient's own hard work. He says this is "your way of thanking [me]" when his patient criticizes him for the absence of food after requesting water. He tells us the gift of water brought up a defense against need and led to disparagement. We also hear his regard through the shared lyrics which speak for themselves. We get a notion of the growth-inducing presence of the over and over again care and interest.

Coen reminds us of the dangers of hating too much, being aroused too much, or being enthralled too much. Only by bringing them into consciousness, can we recognize the signals and manage the conflicts. "A loving, guiding affirming, restraining, appropriately critical superego stance of the analyst at work should be able to manage the Masud Khan in us—some or much, but not all, of the time." Khan struggled to contain his needs, wanting to do his best but unable to transcend his own needs and limitations.

In Safán-Gerard's process, recognition of love includes recognition of separateness and the absent mother. Admitting dependency means risking the loss of 'hard-won autonomy' like Singletary's defense against need and vulnerability. She suggests attacks are out of envy and jealousy for what was missed and was lacking in early relationships. While repairing all damages is impossible, keeping in mind the inherent underlying love eases the enormity of this internal task. She overlooks her patient's statement of his defect which caused harm to his girlfriend. Her consideration of the roots of her oversight is similar to Coen's cited example of McLaughlin (2005) understanding his distance from a male patient through recaptured awareness of his own longings for closeness with a lost father. Safán-Gerard's example describes finding our way back from enactments if we are open to experience our own vulnerabilities. We must tolerate and bear our destructiveness to our own internal objects, which arouses guilt in the analyst for own neglect and abuse of objects. The damaged, unrepaired object in the analyst allows for taking on the projection and failing to help the patient bear the guilt.

For Coen, reverie brings in the edges of consciousness and could prevent such enactments and achieve deeper understanding. He describes a clinical situation in which letting himself in on his hatred of and annoyance with his patient facilitated going after him with active concern. This ability to tolerate our destructiveness through awareness and management is like Singletary's "first aid kit in our hearts for when we hurt, even in our minds, those we love."

Coen's idea of working through identifications with fallen analysts in order to bring our own vulnerabilities into consciousness avoids ganging up against the sane dependent parts of ourselves referred to by Meltzer (1968) and Rosenfeld (1971) in Singletary's contribution. Coen suggests that seamless presentations of clinical material which fail to describe the analyst's struggles convey a mythical image of analytic work which encourages denial and limits access to useful parts of ourselves and hints at analytic omnipotence. Our fear of managing our intense urges prevents that management and puts us at risk of falling prey to them.

Coen's flatness of interpreting his patient's attempts to draw him in negatively is similar to Safán-Gerard's idea of the insufficiency of interpreting the need for punishment or the defense against guilt. Instead, we must help them to bear it. Coen credits accepting his rage with his patient with the subsequent wish to come after his patient not just destructively but also as a way of showing that he cared for him, to insist with him rather than back away and to want him. Wanting to be rid of his patient permanently brought in the desire to tolerate and preserve him in an intimate, authentic relationship. He could then interpret the distance from feelings as he was able to accept his own feelings.

Coen's idea of superego-ishness that is not too harsh and limits access and not too light, risking transgression, is similar to but not as extreme as Singletary's good and bad conscience. As Safán-Gerard describes we must be able to bring in our own destructive tendencies to past and internal objects in order to manage them and avoid the cycle of sadistic response followed by regression to masochistic surrender.

Singletary and Coen bring in use of creative expressions through the play with Singletary's patient and parallels to art. Coen suggests listening for sounds and letting reverie in. Safán-Gerard notes her shock and derailment following fleeting shifts of affect. Singletary introduces love into themes of aggression and destructiveness when he provides loving care for an enemy during play. This care facilitates remorse in his patient's growth. Singletary's patient transforms his creative fantasies into song lyrics which communicate to others his struggles and maturing self-regulation.

Coen lets in wishes to fuck his patient anally or abuse an abused patient. He notes this could risk enactment but not letting it in seems more likely to ensure enactment. This is similar to Safán-Gerard's notion of recognizing our own disturbances in order to let them in rather that remain as split-off mistreatments of our objects. Bringing them into awareness helps us make use of Singletary's first aid kits which contain regard for our patients and more mature ways of managing our feelings. It is the courage to face the painful realities and make the unconscious conscious which makes the work go. Coen and Safán-Gerard remind us this work is ongoing and invite us to use ourselves.

References

Abrams, S. (1990a). Psychoanalytic process: the developmental and the integrative. *Psychoanalytic Quarterly* 59: 650-677.

_____ (1990b). Orienting perspectives on shame and self-esteem. *Psychoanalytic Study of the Child* 45: 411-416.

Akhtar, S. (1996). "Someday . . . " and "if only . . . " fantasies: pathological optimism and inordinate nostalgia as related forms of idealization. *Journal of American Psychoanalytic Association* 44: 723-753.

_____ (2002). Forgiveness: origins, dynamics, psychopathology, and clinical relevance. *Psychoanalytic Quarterly* 71: 175-212.

_____ (2007). Four roadblocks in approaching Masud Khan.*Psychoanalytic Quarterly* 76: 991-995.

_____ (2008). Muslims in the psychoanalytic world. In: *The Crescent and the Couch: Cross-currents between Islam and Psychoanalysis*, ed. S. Akhtar, pp. 315-333. Lanham, MD: Jason Aronson.

_____ (2009). *Comprehensive Dictionary of Psychoanalysis*. London, UK: Karnac Books.

_____ (2011a). *Immigration and Acculturation: Mourning, Adaptation, and the Next Generation*. Lanham, MD: Jason Aronson.

_____ (2011b). Challenges of being an immigrant therapist. In: *Immigration and Acculturation: Mourning, Adaptation, and the Next Generation*, pp. 215-232. Lanham, MD: Jason Aronson.

Akhtar, S., and Choi, L. (2004). When evening falls: the immigrant's encounter with middle and old age. *American Journal of Psychoanalysis* 64: 183-191.

Aligheri, Dante. (1300). *The Divine Comedy Vol. I: Inferno*, transl. M. Musa. New York, NY: Penguin Classics, 1984.

Arieti, S. (1975). *The Will to Be Human*. New York, NY: Dell Publishing.

Armstrong, K. (2005). *A Short History of Myth*. Edinburgh, Scotland: Canongate.

Asch, S. (1976). Varieties of negative therapeutic reactions and problems of technique. *Journal of the American Psychoanalytic Association* 24: 383-407.

Bach, S., and Schwartz, L. (1972). A dream of the Marquis de Sade: psychoanalytic reflections on narcissistic trauma, decompensation, and the reconstitution of a delusional self. *Journal of the American Psychoanalytic Association* 20: 451-475.

Beck, A. T. (1999). *Prisoners of Hate: The Cognitive Basis of Anger, Hostility, and Violence*. New York, NY: HarperCollins.

Bergler, E. (1961). *Curable and Incurable Neurosis: Problems of Neurotic Versus Malignant Masochism*. New York, NY: Liveright.

Bergmann, M. S. (1997). Passions in the therapeutic relationship: a historical perspective. *Canadian Journal of Psychoanalysis* 5: 73-94.

Berliner, B. (1958). The role of object relations in moral masochism. *Psychoanalytic Quarterly* 27: 38-56.

Bernstein, D. (1983). The female superego: a different perspective. *International Journal of Psychoanalysis* 64: 187-201.

Bibring, G. (1954). The training analysis and its place in psychoanalytic training. *International Journal of Psychoanalysis* 35: 169-173.

Blass, R. B. (2012). The ego according to Klein: return to Freud and beyond. *International Journal of Psychoanalysis* 93: 151-165.

Blum, H. (1996). Perspectives on and internalization, consolidation, and change: concluding reflections. In: *The Internal Mother: Conceptual and Technical Aspects of Object Constancy.* eds. S. Akhtar, S. Kramer, and H. Parens, pp. 173-201. Northvale, NJ: Jason Aronson.

Blunt, S.A. (1962). *Artistic Theory in Italy, 1450-1600.* Oxford, UK: Clarendon Press.

Bornstein, B. (1949). The analysis of a phobic child—some problems of theory and technique in child analysis. *Psychoanalytic Study of the Child* 3: 181-226.

Brenner, C. (1959). The masochistic character: genesis and treatment. *Journal of the American Psychoanalytic Association* 7: 197-226.

Buber, M. (1957). Psychiatry. Vol. XX. In: *The Knowledge of Man: Selected Essays.* Amherst, NY: Humanity Books, 1998.

Caper, R. (1997). A mind of one's own. *International Journal of Psychoanalysis* 78: 265-278.

_____ (1998). *A Mind of One's Own: A Kleinian View of Self and Object.* London, UK: Routledge.

Celenza, A. (2007). *Sexual Boundary Violations: Therapeutic, Supervisory, and Academic Contexts.* Lanham, MD: Jason Aronson.

Chodorow, N. (2003). From behind the couch: uncertainty and indeterminacy in psychoanalytic theory and practice. *Common Knowledge* 9: 463-487.

Chused, J. F. and Raphling, D. L. (1992). The analyst's mistakes. *Journal of the American Psychoanalytic Association* 40: 89-116.

Coen, S. J. (1983). Book Review of "Alienation in Perversion" by M. M. R. Khan, 1979. *Journal of the American Psychoanalytic Association* 31: 773-776.

_____ (1985). Perversion as a solution to intrapsychic conflict. *Journal of the American Psychoanalytic Association* 33S: 17-57.

_____ (1994). Barriers to love between patient and analyst. *Journal of the American Psychoanalytic Association* 42: 1107-1135.

_____ (2000). The wish to regress in patient and analyst. *Journal of the American Psychoanalytic Association* 48: 785-810.

_____ (2007). Narcissistic temptations to cross boundaries and how to manage them. *Journal of the American Psychoanalytic Association* 55: 1169-1190.

_____ (2009). Book Review Essay: Reading Memoirs of Childhood: Nathalie Sarraute's "Childhood"; Sarah Kofman's "Rue Ordener, Rue Labat"; Georges Perec's "W, or The Memory of Childhood"; Leo Tolstoy's "Childhood." *International Journal of Psychoanalysis* 90: 145-156.

_____ (2010a, unpublished). Chairman's introduction, Panel: Behind the couch: uses and misuses of temptation. *American Psychoanalytic Association Meetings,* NYC, January 2010.

_____ (2010b). Neediness and narcissistic defensive action. *Psychoanalytic Quarterly* 79: 969-990.

_____ (2010c). Book Review Essay: "Rereading Masud Khan Today: Have His Writings Fallen With Him?" *Journal of the American Psychoanalytic Association* 59: 1005-1020.

Collodi, C. (1991). *The Adventures of Pinocchio: Story of a Puppet,* transl. N. J. Perella. Berkeley, CA: University of California Press.

Cooper, A. (1988). The narcissistic—masochistic character. In: *Masochism: Current Psychoanalytic Perspectives.* eds. R. G. Glick and D. I. Meyers, pp. 117-138. Hillsdale, NJ: Analytic Press.

Covitz, H. (1998). *Oedipal Paradigms in Collision: A Centennial Emendation of a Piece of Freudian Canon (1897-1997).* New York, NY: Peter Lang.

Davis, M. T. (2007). *Jim Dine: Pinocchio.* New York NY: Pace Wildenstein.

Dewald, P. and Clark. R. (2001). eds. Ethics Case Book of the American Psychoanalytic Association. New York, NY: American Psychoanalytic Association.

Disney, W. (1986). *Pinocchio and His Puppet Show Adventure.* Greenwich, CT: Twin Books.

Doidge, N. (2007). *The Brain That Changes Itself: Stories of Personal Triumph from the Frontiers of Brain Science.* New York, NY: Viking.

Eidelberg, L. (ed.). (1968). *Encyclopedia of Psychoanalysis.* New York, NY: Free Press.

Eskelinen de Folch, T. E. (1988). Guilt bearable or unbearable: a problem for the child in analysis. *International Review of Psychoanalysis* 15: 13-24.

Etchegoyen, R. H. (1991). *The Fundamentals of Psychoanalytic Technique.* London, UK: Karnac Books.

Faimberg, H. (1996). Listening to listening. *International Journal of Psychoanalysis* 77: 667-677.

Fraiberg, S. (1982). Pathological defenses in infancy. *Psychoanalytic Quarterly* 51: 612-635.

Fraiberg, S., Edelson, E., and Shapiro V. (1975). Ghosts in the nursery: a psychoanalytic approach to the problems of impaired infant-mother relationships. *Journal of the Academy of Child Psychiatry* 14: 387-421.

Frattaroli, E. J. (1990). A new look at Hamlet: aesthetic response and Shakespeare's meaning. *International Review of Psychoanalysis* 17: 269-285.

_____ (2001). *Healing the Soul in the Age of the Brain: Becoming Conscious in an Unconscious World.* New York, NY: Viking.

_____ (2008). Book review of "Oedipal Paradigms in Collision: A Centennial Emendation of a Piece of Freudian Canon (1897-1997)", by Howard Covitz, 1998. *American Journal of Psychoanalysis* 68: 198-202.

Freud, S. (1905a). Fragment of an analysis of a case of hysteria. *Standard Edition* 7: 1-122.

_____ (1905b). Three essays on the theory of sexuality. *Standard Edition* 7: 135-243.

_____ (1909). Notes upon a case of obsessional neurosis. *Standard Edition* 10: 155-318.

_____ (1912). Recommendations to physicians practicing psycho-analysis. *Standard Edition* 12: 109-120.

_____ (1913a). On beginning the treatment: further recommendations on the technique of psycho-analysis I. *Standard Edition* 12: 121-144.

_____ (1913b).Totem and taboo.*Standard Edition* 13: 1-161.

_____. (1914a). On narcissism: an introduction. *Standard Edition* 14: 67-102.

_____ (1914b). Those wrecked by success. *Standard Edition* 14: 316-331.

_____ (1915a[1914]). Observations on transference love: further recommendations on the technique of psychoanalysis III. *Standard Edition* 12: 157-171.

_____ (1915b). Instincts and their vicissitudes. *Standard Edition* 14: 117-140.

_____ (1916). Some character types met with in psychoanalytic work. *Standard Edition* 14: 310-333.

_____ (1917). The development of the libido and the sexual organizations. *Standard Edition* 16: 320-338.

_____ (1919). The 'uncanny.'*Standard Edition* 17: 217-252.

_____ (1920). Beyond the pleasure principle. *Standard Edition* 18: 7-64.

_____ (1923). The ego and the id. *Standard Edition* 18: 235-259.

_____ (1924a). The dissolution of the Oedipus complex. *Standard Edition* 19: 171-188.

_____ (1924b). The economic problem of masochism. *Standard Edition* 19: 157-170.

_____ (1925). Some psychical consequences of the anatomical distinction between the sexes. *Standard Edition* 19: 241-258.

_____ (1930). Civilization and its discontents. *Standard Edition* 21: 57-146.

_____ (1937). Analysis terminable and interminable. *Standard Edition* 23: 209-254.

Friedman, H. H. (2007, unpublished). Discussion of "Narcissistic temptations to cross boundaries and how to manage them" by S.J. Coen. *American Psychoanalytic Association Meetings,* January, 2007.

Friedman, L. (1991). A reading of Freud's papers on technique. *Psychoanalytic Quarterly* 60: 564-595.

Gabbard, G. O. (1994). On love and lust in erotic transference. *Journal of the American Psychoanalytic Association* 42: 385-403.

_____ (1995). The early history of boundary violations in psychoanalysis.*Journal of the American Psychoanalytic Association* 43: 1115-1136.

Gabbard, G. O., and Lester, E. (1995). *Boundaries and Boundary Violations in Psychoanalysis*. New York, NY: Basic Books.

Gaylin, W. (1990). *Adam and Eve and Pinocchio: On Being and Becoming Human*. New York, NY: Viking.

Gediman, H., and Wolkenfeld, F. (1980). The parallelism phenomenon in psychoanalysis and supervision: its reconsideration as a triadic system. *Psychoanalytic Quarterly* 49: 234-255.

Gilligan, C. (1982). *In a Different Voice: Psychological Theory and Women's Development*. Cambridge, MA: Harvard University Press.

Goldberg, A. (2003). *Errant Selves: A Casebook of Misbehavior*. Hillsdale, NJ: The Analytic Press.

_____ (2007). *Moral Stealth*. Chicago, IL: University of Chicago Press.

Goldman, D. (2006). The outrageous prince: Winnicott's un-cure of Masud Khan. Paper presented at N.Y.U. Postdoctoral Program in Psychology.

Gooch, J. (1992). Personal communication.

Grinberg, L. (1964). Two kinds of guilt—their relations with normal and pathological aspects of mourning. *International Journal of Psychoanalysis* 45: 366-371.

_____ (1978). The 'razors edge' in depression and mourning. *International Journal of Psychoanalysis* 59: 245-254.

_____ (1992). *Guilt and Depression*. London, UK: Karnac Books.

Grinker, R. (1955). Growth inertia and shame: their therapeutic implications and dangers. *International Journal of Psychoanalysis* 36: 242-253.

Gross, K. (2011). *Puppet: An essay on uncanny life*. Chicago, IL: University of Chicago Press.

Guroian, V. (1998). *Tending the Heart of Virtue: How Classic Stories Awaken a Child's Moral Imagination*. New York, NY: Oxford University Press.

Harris, A. (2009). "You must remember this." *Psychoanalytic Dialogues* 19: 2–21.

Harris and Sinsheimer (2008). The analyst's vulnerability: preserving and fine-tuning analytic bodies. In: *Bodies in Treatment: The Unknown Dimension*, ed. F.S. Anderson, pp. 255-274. New York, NY: Taylor and Francis.

Heaney, S. (2002). *Finders Keepers: Selected Prose, 1971-2001*. London, UK: Faber.

Hebb, D. O. (1949). *The Organization of Behavior: A Neuropsychological Theory*. New York, NY: John Wiley and Sons.

Helt, M., Kelley, E., Kinsbourne, M., Pandey, J., Boorstein, H., Herbert, M., and Fein, D. (2008). Can children with autism recover? If so, how? *Neuropsychology Review* 18: 339-366.

Hertz, N. (1985). *The End of the Line*. Aurora, CO: The Davies Group, 2009.

Hirsch, I. (2008). *Coasting in the Countertransference: Conflicts of Self Interest between Analyst and Patient*. New York, NY: The Analytic Press.

Hoffer, W. (1955). *Psychoanalysis: Practical and Research Aspects*. Baltimore, MD: Williams and Wilkins.

Hoffman, L. (2007). Do children get better when we interpret their defenses against painful feelings? *Psychoanalytic Study of the Child* 62: 291-313.

Hoffman, M. (2004). From enemy combatant to strange bedfellow: the role of religious narratives in the work of W. R. D. Fairbairn and D. W. Winnicott. *Psychoanalytic Dialogues* 14: 769-804.

Holmes, D. E. (2006). The wrecking effects of race and social class on self and success. *Psychoanalytic Quarterly* 75: 215-235.

Hopkins, L. (2006). *False Self: The Life of Masud Khan*. New York, NY: Other Press.

Hughes, D. A. (1997). *Facilitating Developmental Attachment: The Road to Emotional Recovery and Behavioral Change in Foster and Adopted Children*. Northvale, NJ: Jason Aronson.

Hurvich, M. (2003). The place of annihilation anxieties in psychoanalytic theo-ry.*Journal of the American Psychoanalytic Association* 51: 579-616.

Imber, R.R. (1995). The role of the pregnant analyst and the supervisor. *Psychoanalytic Psychology* 12: 281-296.

_____ (1998). Modifying the analyst's superego. *Contemporary Psychoanalysis* 34: 577-582.

Jacobs (2006). Review of "The Healer's Bent: Solitude and Dialogue in the Clinical Encounter." by James T. McLaughlin. *Journal of the American Psychoanalytic Association* 54: 1422-1426.

Jaques, E. (1967). Guilt, conscience and social behavior. In: *Work, Creativity and Social Justice*, pp. 167-180. London, UK: Heinemann, 1970.

Jones, E. (1929). Fear, guilt, and hate. *International Journal of Psychoanalysis* 10: 383-397.

Joseph, B. (1983). On understanding and not understanding: some technical issues. In: *Psychic Equilibrium and Psychic Change*, pp. 139-150. London, UK: Routledge, 1989.

Kanwal, G. S. (2010). Book review of "Loving Psychoanalysis: Technique and Theory in the Therapeutic Relationship", by S.S. Levine. *International Journal of Psychoanalysis* 91: 219-222.

Kernberg, O. (1975). *Borderline Conditions and Pathological Narcissism*. New York, NY: Jason Aronson.

Khan, M. M. R. (1965). The function of intimacy and acting out in perversions. In: *Sexual Behavior and the Law*, ed. R. Slovenko, pp. 397-412. Springfield, IL: Thomas.

_____ (1969). Role of the "collated internal object" in perversion-formations. *International Journal of Psychoanalysis* 50: 555-565.

_____ (1981). "La main mauvaise". *Nouvelle Revue de Psychoanalyse* 24: 5-51.

Kilbourne, B. (2005). Shame conflicts and tragedy in "The Scarlet Letter". *Journal of the American Psychoanalytic Association* 53: 465-483.

Kitayama, O. (1997) Psychoanalysis in shame culture. *The Bulletin* 85: 47-50.

Kite, J. (2008). Ideas of influence: the impact of the analyst's character on the analysis. *Psychoanalytic Quarterly* 77: 1075-1104.

Klein, G.S. (1976). *Psychoanalytic Theory: An Exploration of Essentials*. New York: International Universities Press.

Klein, M. (1933). The early development of conscience in the child. In: *Love, Guilt and Reparation and Other Works 1921-1945*, pp. 248-258. New York, NY: The Free Press, 1984.

_____ (1935). A contribution to the psychogenesis of manic depressive states. In: *Love, Guilt and Reparation and Other Works—1921-1945*, pp. 262-289. New York, NY: Free Press, 1975.

_____ (1937). Love, guilt, and reparation. In: *Love, Guilt and Reparation and Other Works—1921-1945*, pp. 306-343. New York, NY: Free Press, 1975.

_____ (1940). Mourning and its relation to manic depressive states. In: *Love, Guilt and Reparation and Other Works—1921-1945*, pp. 344-369. New York, NY: Free Press, 1975.

_____ (1946). Notes on some schizoid mechanisms. In: *The Selected Melanie Klein*, ed. J. Mitchell, pp. 175-200. New York, NY: Free Press, 1986.

_____ (1948). On the theory of anxiety and guilt. In: *Envy and Gratitude and Other Works—1946-1963*, pp. 25-42. London, UK: Hogarth Press, 1975.

_____ (1957). Envy and gratitude. In: *The Writings of Melanie Klein, Volume 3, Envy and Gratitude and Other Works, 1946-1963*, pp. 176-235. New York, NY: The Free Press, 1984.

_____ (1960). A note on depression in the schizophrenic. In: *Envy and Gratitude and Other Works—1946-1963*, pp. 264-267. London, UK: Hogarth Press, 1975.

Kohut, H. (1972). Thoughts on narcissism and narcissistic rage. *Psychoanalytic Study of the Child* 27: 360-400.

Krafft-Ebing, R. (1892). *Psychopathia Sexualis with Special Reference to Contrary Sexual Instinct: a Medico-legal Study*. Philadelphia, PA: F.A. Davis Press, 1978.

Kristeva, J. (1982). *Powers of Horror*. New York, NY: Columbia University Press.

_____ (1996). *New Maladies of the Soul*. New York, NY: Columbia University Press.

Kumar, M. (2007). Review of "Masud Khan: The Myth and the Reality", by Roger Willoughby. *Psychoanalytic Quarterly* 76: 997-1008.

Lacan, J. (1949). The mirror stage as formative of the I function as revealed in psychoanalytic experience. In: *Ecrits*, pp. 1-7, transl. B. Fink. New York, NY: W.W. Norton, 2002.

Laplanche, J. (1999). Notes on afterwardsness. In: *Essays on Otherness*, pp. 260-265, transl. J. Fletcher. London, UK: Routledge.

Laplanche, J., and Pontalis, J. B. (1973). *The Language of Psychoanalysis*, trans. D. Nicholson-Smith. New York, NY: W.W. Norton.

Lasky, R. (1992). Some superego conflicts in the analyst who has suffered a catastrophic illness. *International Journal of Psychoanalysis* 73: 127-136.

Levin, S. (1967). Some metapsychological considerations on the differentiation between shame and guilt. *International Journal of Psychoanalysis* 48: 267-276.

Levine, S. (2010). *Loving Psychoanalysis: Technique and Theory in the Therapeutic Relationship*. Lanham, MD: Jason Aronson.

Lewis, M. D. (2005). Self-organizing individual differences in brain development. *Developmental Review* 25: 252-277.

Loewald, H.W. (1960). On the therapeutic action of psychoanalysis. *Journal of the American Psychoanalytic Association* 41: 16-33.

_____ (1962). Internalization, separation, mourning, and the superego.*Psychoanalytic Quarterly* 31: 483-504

Mahler, M. S., Pine, F., and Bergman, A. (1975). *The Psychological Birth of the Human Infant: Symbiosis and Individuation*. New York, NY: Basic Books.

Maleson, F. (1984). Multiple meanings of masochism in psychoanalytic discourse. *Journal of the American Psychoanalytic Association* 32: 325-356.

Mason, A. (1995). Personal communication.

McLaughlin, J. T. (2005). *The Healer's Bent: Solitude and Dialogue in the Clinical Encounter*. Hillsdale, NJ: The Analytic Press.

Meltzer, D. (1968). Terror, persecution, dread. *International Journal of Psychoanalysis* 49: 396-411.

Meyer, B.C. (1967). *Joseph Conrad*. Princeton, NJ: Princeton University Press.

_____ (1972). Some reflections on the contributions of psychoanalysis to biography. *Psychoanalysis and Contemporary Science* 1: 373-391.

Mish, F .C. (ed.), (1998). *Merriam Webster's Collegiate Dictionary* (10th Edition). Springfield, MA: Merriam Webster Press.

Modell, A. (1965). On aspects of the superego's development. *International Journal of Psychoanalysis* 46: 323-331.

Money-Kyrle, R. E. (1956). Normal counter-transference and some of its deviations.*International Journal of Psychoanalysis* 37: 360-366.

Moore, B. and Fine, B. (1990).*Psychoanalytic Terms and Concepts*. New Haven, CT: Yale University Press.

Morrison, A. (1989). *Shame, the Underside of Narcissism*. Hillsdale, NJ: The Analytic Press.

Niederland, W. (1968). Clinical observations on the 'survivor syndrome.' *International Journal of Psychoanalysis* 49: 313-315.

Novick, J., and Novick, K. K. (2001). Two systems of self-regulation.*Psychoanalytic Social Work* 8: 95-122.

Novick, K. K., and Novick, J. (2003). Two systems of self-regulation and the differential application of psychoanalytic technique. *American Journal of Psychoanalysis* 63: 1-20.

_____ (2012). Building emotional muscle in children and parents.*Psychoanalytic Study of the Child* 65: 131-151.

Ogden, T. (1994). The analytic third: working with intersubjective clinical facts. *International Journal of Psychoanalysis* 75: 3-19.

_____ (1997a). Reverie and metaphor: some thoughts on how I work as a psychoanalyst. *International Journal of Psychoanalysis* 78: 719-732.

_____ (1997b). Reverie and interpretation. In: *Reverie and Interpretation: Sensing Something Human*, pp. 155-197. Northvale, NJ: Jason Aronson.

Olinick, S. L., Poland, W. S., Grigg, K. A., and Granatir, W. L. (1973). The psychoanalytic work ego: process and interpretation. *International Journal of Psychoanalysis* 54: 143-151.

Ornstein, A. (1974). The dread to repeat and the new beginning: a contribution to the psychoanalysis of the narcissistic personality disorders. *Annual of Psychoanalysis* 2: 231-248.

O'Shaughnessey, E. (1981). A clinical study of a defensive organization.*International Journal of Psychoanalysis* 62: 359-369.

Panel, (2006). Sexual boundary violations in analytic work: three perspectives. *Association for Psychoanalytic Medicine*, N.Y.C., April, 2006.

Panel, (2009/2010). Rereading Masud Khan today: have his writings fallen with him? *Association for Psychoanalytic Medicine*, N.Y.C., December, 2009. San Francisco Psychoanalytic Society, San Francisco CA, December, 2010

Panel, (2010). Behind the couch: uses and misuses of temptation. *American Psychoanalytic Association Meetings*, N.Y.C., January, 2010.

Parens, H. (1979).*The Development of Aggression in Early Childhood*. New York, NY: Jason Aronson.

Parsons, M. (2000). *The Dove that Returns, the Dove that Vanishes: Paradox and Creativity in Psychoanalysis*. London, UK: Routledge.

Parsons, M. (2006). The analyst's countertransference to the psychoanalytic process. *International Journal of Psychoanalysis* 87: 1183-1198.

_____ (2007). Raiding the inarticulate: the internal analytic setting and listening beyond countertransference. *International Journal of Psychoanalysis* 88: 1441-1456.

Perella, N. (1986). An essay on Pinocchio [Introduction]. In: *The Adventures of Pinocchio: Story of a Puppet*, C. Collodi. transl. N. Perella, pp. 1-69. Berkeley, CA: University of California Press.

Perkins, W. (1966). *His Pioneer Works on Casuistry: A Discourse of Conscience and The Whole Treatise of Cases of Conscience*. ed. T. F. Merrill. Niewkoop, Netherlands: B. de Graaf.

Pine, F. (1997).*Diversity and Direction in Psychoanalytic technique*. New Haven, CT: Yale University Press.

Pinocchio (1940). A Walt Disney Production. N. Ferguson, Director.

Pinocchio (2002). A Melampo Cinematographie/Miramax Production. Begnini, R., Director.

Pinsky, R. (2006). 'In Depth with Robert Pinsky', moderated by S. J. Coen. *American Psychoanalytic Association Meetings*, New York City.

Poland, W. (2006). The analyst's fear.*American Imago* 63: 201-217.

Racker, H. (1968) *Transference and Counter-Transference*. London, UK: Hogarth Press.

Reich, W. (1933). Character Analysis. transl. V. R. Carfagno. New York, NY: Farrar, Strauss, and Giroux, 1972.

Rey, H. (1986). Reparation. *Journal of the Melanie Klein Society* 4: 5-35.

_____ (1988). That which patients bring to analysis, *International Journal of Psychoanalysis* 69: 457-470.

Riesenberg, R. (1981). Expiation as a defense. *International Journal of Psychoanalytic Psychotherapy* 8: 549-570.

Rosenbloom, S. (1992). The development of the work ego in the beginning analyst: thoughts on identity formation in the psychoanalyst. *International Journal of Psychoanalysis* 73 117-126.

Rosenfeld, H. (1964). On the psychopathology of narcissism: a clinical approach. In: *Psychotic States: A Psychoanalytic Approach*. London, UK: Hogarth Press, 1965.

_____ (1971). A clinical approach to the psychoanalytic theory of the life and death instincts: an investigation into the aggressive aspects of narcissism. *International Journal of Psychoanalysis* 52: 169-178.

Rycroft, C. (1968). *A Critical Dictionary of Psychoanalysis*. London, UK: Penguin Books, 1972.

Safán-Gerard, D. (1998). Bearable and unbearable guilt: a Kleinian perspective. *Psychoanalytic Quarterly* 67: 351-378.

Said, E. W. (2003).*Freud and the Non-European*. London, UK: Verso.

Schafer, R. (1960). The loving and beloved superego in Freud's structural theory.*Psychoanalytic Study of the Child* 15: 163-188.

_____ (1977).The interpretation of transference and the conditions of loving.*Journal of the American Psychoanalytic Association* 25: 355-362.

_____ (1983). *The Analytic Attitude*. New York, NY: Basic Books.

_____ (1993). Five readings of Freud's "Observations on transference love". In: *On Freud's "Observations on Transference Love"*. ed. E.S. Person, A. Hagelin, and P. Fonagy, pp. 75-95. New Haven, CT: Yale University Press.

Schmideberg, M. (1938). "After the analysis". *Psychoanalytic Quarterly* 7: 122-142.

Searles, H. F. (1963). The place of neutral therapist-responses in psychotherapy with the schizophrenic patient. *International Journal of Psychoanalysis* 44:42-56.

_____ (1986). *My Work with Borderline Patients*. Northvale, NJ: Jason Aronson.

Segal, H. (1952). A psycho-analytical approach to aesthetics.*International Journal of Psychoanalysis* 33: 196-207.

_____ (1974).*Introduction to the Work of Melanie Klein*. New York, NY: Basic Books.

_____ (1981). Manic reparation. In: *The Work of Hanna Segal*, pp. 147-158. London, UK: Jason Aronson.

Settlage, C. (1992). Psychoanalytic observations on adult development and life and in the therapeutic relationship. *Psychoanalysis and Contemporary Thought* 15: 349-374.

Shakespeare, W. (1595). *A Midsummer Night's Dream*. London, UK: Methuen, 1979.

Shengold, L. (2004). A brief psychoanalytic note on Wordsworth, poetic creativity, and love.*American Poetry Review*, January/February: 27-29.

Shill, M. A. (2004). Analytic neutrality, anonymity, abstinence, and elective self-disclosure. *Journal of the American Psychoanalytic Association* 52: 151-187.

Silverman, D. (personal communication, 12/09, in response to panel "Rereading Masud Khan Today: Have His Writings Fallen With Him?" *Association for Psychoanalytic Medicine*, N.Y.C., December, 2009.

Singletary, W. (2000). *Emotional Diabetes: A Syndrome of Hostile Self and Object Constancy*. Presented at the Meetings of the American Psychoanalytic Association: The Vulnerable Child Workshop. Chicago, IL, May.

_____ (2001). Changing hateful feelings back to loving feelings: the work of child analysis—discussion of Herbert Schlesinger's presentation, "Technical Problems in Analyzing the Mourning Patient. In: *Three Faces of Mourning: Melancholia, Manic Defense, and Moving On*. ed. S. Akhtar, pp. 141-156. Northvale, NJ: Jason Aronson.

_____ (2005). The internal monster: An aspect of hostile self and object constancy— discussion of Tyson's chapter, "Separation-Individuation, Object Constancy, and Affect Regulation. In: *The Language of Emotions: Development, Psychopathology, and Technique*. eds. S. Akhtar and H. Blum, pp. 83-96. Lanham, MD: Jason Aronson.

_____ (2007). *Safety or Danger: a Reconsideration of the Concept of Object Constancy*. Lecture presented at a special program in honor of Dr. Anni Bergman, sponsored by The Institute for Psychoanalytic Training and Research. New York, New York, November 16.

Slochower, J. (2006). *Psychoanalytic Collisions*. Mahwah, NJ: The Analytic Press.

_____ (2010). Unpublished: Analytic asymmetry and collisions of idealization. Presented at *American Psychoanalytic Association Panel*, "Behind the couch: uses and misuses of temptation", January 2010.

Spero, M. H. (1984). Shame—an object-relational formation. *Psychoanalytic Study of the Child* 39: 259-282.

Spielrein, S. (1912). *Die DestruktionalsUrsache des Werdens. Jahrbuchpsychoanal.psychopathol. Forsch.* 4, 1912, 465-503. English translation: Destruction as the cause of coming into being. *Journal of Analytic Psychology* 39: 155-186, 1994.

Steiner, J. (1987) The interplay between pathological organizations and the paranoid-schizoid and depressive positions. *International Journal of Psychoanalysis* 68: 69-80.

_____ (1990). Pathological organizations as obstacles to mourning: the role of unbearable guilt. *International Journal of Psychoanalysis* 71: 87-94.

_____ (2000). Book review of "A Mind of One's Own: A Kleinian View of Self and Object", by Robert Caper. *Journal of the American Psychoanalytic Association* 48: 637-643.

Sterba, R. (1934). The fate of the ego in analytic therapy.*International Journal of Psychoanalysis* 15: 117-126.

Stern, D. (2010). *Partners in Thought: Working with Unformulated Experience, Dissociation, and Enactment.* New York, NY: Routledge.

Stone, J. (1994). Pinocchio and Pinocchiology.*American Imago* 51: 329-342.

Stone, L. (1961). *The Psychoanalytic Situation.* New York, NY: International Universities Press.

Strachey, J. (1934). The nature of the therapeutic action of psycho-analysis. *International Journal of Psychoanalysis* 15: 127-159.

Sullivan, H.S. (1953). *The Interpersonal Theory of Psychiatry.* New York, NY: W.W. Norton.

Summers, F. (2001). What I do with what you give me: therapeutic action as the creation of meaning. *Psychoanalytic Psychology* 18: 635-655.

Tayler, E. W. (2011, unpublished). Antony and Cleopatra: to love or die? University Forum: Shakespeare's "Antony and Cleopatra". *American Psychoanalytic Association Meetings,* New York, NY.

Viorst, J. (1982). Experience of loss at the end of analysis.*Psychoanalytic Inquiry:* 2: 399-418.

Volkan, V. (1987). Psychological concepts useful in the building of political foundations between nations (Track II diplomacy). *Journal of the American Psychoanalytic Association* 35: 903-935.

Waelder, R. (1930). The principle of multiple function: observations on overdetermination. In: *Psychoanalysis: Observation, Theory, Application.* ed. S. A. Guttman, pp. 68-83. New York, NY: International Universities Press, 1976.

_____ (1965).*Psychoanalytic Avenues to Art.* New York: International Universities Press.

Weiss, J. M. A. (1974). Suicide. In: *American Handbook of Psychiatry,* 2nd Edition, Volume 3. eds. S. Arieti and E. B. Brody, pp. 743-765. New York, NY: Basic Books.

Wilson, M. (2003). The analyst's desire and the problem of narcissistic resistances.*Journal of the American Psychoanalytic Association* 51: 71-99.

Winnicott, D. W. (1949). Hate in the countertransference. *International Journal of Psychoanalysis* 30: 69-74.

_____ (1960). Ego distortion in terms of true and false self. In *The Maturational Processes and the Facilitating Environment: Studies in the Theory of Emotional Development.* London: Hogarth Press, 1965, 140-152.

_____ (1968). The use of an object and relating through identifications. In: *Playing and Reality,* pp. 86-94. London, UK: Tavistock.

_____ (1971). *Playing and Reality.* London: Tavistock Publications.

_____ (1971). Mirror-role of the mother and family in child development. In: *Playing and Reality,* pp. 111-118. London, UK: Routledge, 1989.

Wurmser, L. (1994). *The Mask of Shame.* Northvale, NJ: Jason Aronson.

_____ (2007). *"Torment Me, But Don't Abandon Me": Psychoanalysis of the Severe Neurosis in a New Key.* Lanham, MD: Rowman and Littlefield.

Index

99–100, 104, 107, 108–109; primary narcissism and, 34; superego and, 95, 96; *The Uncanny*, 32, 34, 36, 39n1; unconscious guilt for, 42, 112, 116
Frost, Robert, 82n4
furor sanandi (rage to cure), 102

Gabbard, G.O., 69, 119
gender, 13
Germany, 13
Golden Rule, 91, 94, 105
good, 29
gratification, 33
gratitude, 51
Growing Up, 25
guilt, definition of, 2–3. *See also specific entries*

Harris, 82n3
hatred, 9; love and, 41, 116; towards object, 57; for psychoanalysis, 76
Heaney, S., 72
Hebb's Law, 19
heimlich (homely), 32
helpful guilt, 26
Hertz, Neil, 35
Hirsch, Irwin, 80
Hoffer, W., 19
Hoffman, M., 93, 94
Holland, 13
Holocaust survivors, 8
homely *(heimlich)*, 32
homeostasis, 107

I am sorry, 1
id, 31
idealization, 57
I-It relationship, 92, 93, 104, 108, 109
immigrants, 7, 8
imposing-on, 92, 93
The Imprisoned Analysand (Schafer), 20
imprisonment, 20, 23, 27, 114; creativity about, 24; transference, 43
inadequacy, 2
individuality, 90
induced guilt, 8
infant, 4
The Inferno (Dante), 20
infidelity, 45, 66

intellectualization, 46, 50, 120
internalization, 2
interpretation, 4–14, 18, 116–117; of defenses, 27, 31, 112; as distraction, 122; primary focus in, 57; with transference, 43, 77–78
Italy, 13
I-Thou relationship, 91–92, 93, 94, 104, 105, 108, 109

Jacobs, 70, 74
Japan, 13
Jones, E., 9
justice system, 13

Kanwal, G.S., 76
Khan, Masud, 81–82, 122
Kite, J., 120
Klein, Melanie, 4, 30; language of, 29; morality for, 106; Oedipus complex for, 31; reparation for, 42, 112
von Krafft-Ebing, R., 11
Kristeva, Julia, 37, 39

Lacan, J., 34, 34–35
language, 29
Laplanche, J., 34, 35, 39
"Last Night," 36
Lester, E., 69, 119
"Let Me Out," 24
Levine, S.S., 76
Lewis, M.D., 19
Loewald, H.W., 121
loss, 19, 27
love: capacity for, 67; *caritas*, 17; devaluing of, 57; guilt from, 44, 48, 117; hatred and, 41, 116; mobilization of, 41, 57; morality in, 87, 105; object constancy and, 19; for psychoanalysis, 75–76; in psychoanalysis, 17–18, 29, 114; in transference, 114

Mach, Ernst, 36
Mahler, Margaret, 19, 34, 113
manic defenses, 12, 42, 54, 55
manipulation, 49
masochism, 11–12, 14n4, 52. *See also* sadomasochism

About the Editor and Contributors

Salman Akhtar, M.D., Professor of Psychiatry, Jefferson Medical College; Training and Supervising Analyst, Psychoanalytic Center of Philadelphia, Philadelphia, PA.

Jeanne Bailey, Ph.D., Training and Supervising Analyst, Minnesota Psychoanalytic Society, Minneapolis, MN.

Stanley J. Coen, M.D., Clinical Professor of Psychiatry, College of Physicians, Surgeons, Columbia University; Training and Supervising Analyst, Columbia University Center for Psychoanalytic Training and Research, New York, NY.

Elio Frattaroli, M.D., Faculty Member, Psychoanalytic Center of Philadelphia; private practice of psychotherapy and psychoanalysis, Bala Cynwyd, PA.

Desy Safán-Gerard, Ph.D., Training and Supervising Analyst, Psychoanalytic Center of California, Los Angeles, CA.

Robert Kravis, Psy.D., Faculty Member, Psychoanalytic Center of Philadelphia; private practice of adult and child psychotherapy and psychoanalysis, Philadelphia, PA.

William R. Singletary, M.D., President, Margaret S. Mahler Psychiatric Research Foundation; Faculty, Psychoanalytic Center of Philadelphia; private practice of adult and child psychotherapy and psychoanalysis, Ardmore, PA.

Elaine Zickler, Ph.D., Faculty Member, Psychoanalytic Center of Philadelphia; private practice of psychotherapy and psychoanalysis, Philadelphia, PA.